Samuel

Samuel

the Prophet

F. B. Meyer

CLC ❖ PUBLICATIONS
Fort Washington, Pennsylvania 19034

Published by CLC ❖ Publications

U.S.A.
P.O. Box 1449, Fort Washington, PA 19034

GREAT BRITAIN
51 The Dean, Alresford, Hants. SO24 9BJ

AUSTRALIA
P.O. Box 419M, Manunda, QLD 4879

NEW ZEALAND
10 MacArthur Street, Feilding

ISBN 0-87508-339-0

This American edition published by
CLC Publications,
Fort Washington, PA.

This printing 2002

Printed in the United States of America

CONTENTS

Chapter   Page

1. An Age of Transition. 7
2. A Woman's Anguish of Heart 15
3. The Young Levite 23
4. The Vision of God 31
5. Misfortune on Misfortune 39
6. The Work of Reconstruction 51
7. The Victory of Faith 55
8. The Stone of Help 63
9. A Great Disappointment 69
10. The Voice of Circumstances 81
11. As Occasion Serves. 87
12. The Inner and Outer Conflicts 95
13. Forsaken? Never! 105
14. Not Ceasing in Prayer. 115
15. The Causes of Saul's Downfall 123
16. "Two Putting Ten Thousand to Flight" 131
17. Failure Under the Supreme Test 139
18. A Remarkable Colloquy 147
19. "An Evil Spirit from the Lord" 155
20. "Sin Bringing Forth Death" 165
21. The Sin of Jealousy 173
22. "Cruel as the Grave" 181
23. A Great Sunset. 191
24. Endor and Gilboa 201
25. An Epilogue. 211

1

AN AGE OF TRANSITION

(1 Samuel 1)

"The old order changeth, yielding place to new,
And God fulfills himself in many ways,
Lest one good custom should corrupt the world."

TENNYSON

"ON WHOM the ends of the ages are come"—i.e., the end of one age and the beginning of another. Such is our position today. In every direction the old order is giving place to the new. It was thus in the days of the primitive Church, when the typical institutions of the Levitical system were being replaced by "the heavenly things themselves." And it was also thus at the time when our narrative begins. The story of Samuel is a divine interlude between the days of the judges and those of David the King.

Hitherto the high priesthood had been the supreme authority recognized in the Hebrew commonwealth. To Moses, its founder, there could be of course no successor; but Aaron was the first of an unbroken line of priests. No other office stood for the whole of Israel. The Mosaic era, however, was not destined to culminate in the *rule* of the priest, who has seldom combined the sacerdotal functions with the special qualifications that constitute a great leader and ruler. Too often the reign of the churchman has been warped by bigotry, tyranny, and the repression of the nobler aspirations of mankind. The priest was to make way for the king.

A suggestion that a fresh development of the Hebrew polity was near occurs in the closing verses of the book of Ruth, with which the book of First Samuel is connected by the conjunction *now*. The genealogy which is the evident climax, and with which that sweet pastoral story closes, has no connection with Aaron or his line. It expressly deals with the tribe of Judah, of which nothing was spoken concerning the priesthood. Evidently the divine purpose was moving forward—but whither? At the time its goal was not apparent; but as we look back on all the circumstances from the vantage ground of accomplished fact, we can see that it was slowly moving towards the establishment of the kingdom under David. And, veiled from all eyes, there was the yet profounder movement towards the revelation of "that Proper Man" (as Luther calls Him) in whose nature—fitly known as Wonderful—the priestly, the prophetic, and the royal *blend* in perfect symmetry and beauty.

I. THE URGENT NEED FOR A STRONG MAN.—Every age takes up and provokes the cry "Give us men." But if ever a strong man was needed, it was in the days of which the book of Judges affords some startling glimpses.

Canaan had been conquered, but the ancient inhabitants were far from being subdued; they remained much as the Saxons did under the early Norman kings. In the South, the Philistines held their five cities. The mountain fortress which was afterwards known as Mount Zion, garrisoned by Jebusites, was proudly defiant as far forward as the days of David. Nearly all the seacoast, and all the strongholds in the rich plain of Esdraelon, were in the hands of the Canaanites. The little kingdom of Gezer remained independent till it was conquered by the King of Egypt and given as a dowry to Solomon's queen. On the northern frontier were the remains of those mighty nations which Joshua had overthrown in the great battle of the Waters of Merom, but which probably only gave a nominal allegiance to the Israelite suzerainty. "So the Lord left those nations, without driving them out hastily, . . . to prove Israel by them, even as many as had not known the wars of Canaan, . . . to teach them war, at the least such as before time knew nothing thereof." Had it not been for the presence of these warlike tribes, we would never have heard of Gideon, of Barak, of Jephthah, of Samson, or of David. Without this discipline, Israel might have become an effeminate and molluscous race, lacking backbone and muscle. They would have dwelt in security after the manner of the Sidonians—quiet and secure in a large land, a place where there was no lack of anything that is in the earth (Judges 2:23–3:2; 18:7,10).

How often in our earthly discipline we come into experiences which are the counterpart of these. There are wars where we looked for peace; fret and chafe where we expected freedom from annoyance; pouring from vessel to vessel where we hoped to be allowed to settle on our lees. Are not these clearly permitted to try us, that we may learn war; that we may know ourselves and know God; that we and our children may grow up into a nobler and healthier style of character than had otherwise been possible?

In Israel this incessant exposure to attack was aggravated by the absence of a strong central government. The priesthood had evidently fallen into the hands of weaklings from the days of Phinehas. Of this there is striking confirmation in the fact that Eli sprang not from the house of Eleazar, the eldest son of Aaron, in which the succession ought to have been continued, but from the family of the younger son, Ithamar. There is a strong probability that the representatives of the elder branch had proved themselves so unable to cope with the disorders of the time that they had been set aside in favor of anyone who evinced faculty enough to take the field and marshal the forces of Israel. Perhaps Eli, in his young life, had done some stirring deed of prowess which raised him to the supreme position his fellow countrymen could give; though, when we are introduced to him, he is pitiful in his senile decrepitude and weakness (1 Chron. 6:4–15; 24:4).

From time to time captains had been raised up as a temporary expedient. "He gave them judges until Samuel the prophet." "And when the Lord raised up judges, then the Lord was with the judge, and saved them out of the hand of their enemies all the days of the judge; for it repented the Lord because of their groaning by reason of them that oppressed them and vexed them" (Acts 13:20; Judges 2:18). The reign of a judge was, however, a very transient gleam of light in that dark and stormy age. At the furthest, his power was only recognized within his own and the adjacent tribes. Samson, for instance, was little else than the hero of the south country, while Jephthah was preeminently the captain of the trans-Jordanic tribes. In many cases the office ceased with the special crisis that called it into being. Only in the case of two or three, such as Deborah and Gideon, did conspicuous service lead to a lifelong primacy.

Thus the nation was in danger of desolation by internal anarchy and external attack. With no principle of cohesion, no rallying-point, no acknowledged leader, what was there to resist the pressure of the Canaanites from within and of the hostile nations from without its borders? "In those days there was no king in Israel, but every man did that which was right in his own eyes"; "The children of Israel did evil in the sight of the Lord"; "The children of Israel cried unto the Lord." These three sentences, repeated frequently and emphatically, are the keynotes of the whole book. The religious ties, moreover, were very weak. We find, for instance, the name of Baal, a Phoenician deity, occurring three times in the names of members of the family of Saul (1 Chron. 8:30, 33–34). The stories of Micah, of Ruth, and of the extermination carried out by the Danites, supply graphic pictures of the disunion, independence, and wildness of the time—of wild license, and of exposure to attack.

It was necessary, therefore, to introduce a new order of things. To assert and achieve the national unity; to make the best aspects of the rule of the judges permanent in the office of kingship; to resuscitate and maintain the allegiance of Israel to the God of their fathers; to carry over the whole nation from the time of the last judge to that of the first king—was a task that demanded a preeminently strong man; and the need was superbly supplied, as we shall see, by the prophet Samuel, who conducted his people from one age to another without a revolution, and almost without the excitement which naturally accompanies so great a change.

II. HOW THE NEED WAS MET.—God's greatest gifts to man come through travail. Whether we look into the spiritual or the temporal sphere, can we discover anything—any great reform, any beneficent discovery, any soul-awakening revival—which did not come through the toils and tears, the vigils and bloodshedding of men and women whose sufferings were the pangs of its birth? That which costs nothing is of small avail to the salvation and help of mankind. The souls that are set on saving *themselves* will never be the saviors of the race. If the temple is to be raised, David must bear sore afflictions; if the gospel of the grace of God is to be disentangled from Jewish tradition, Paul's life must be one long agony. If the Reformation is to be rendered possible for Europe, men like John Huss and Jerome must be burned at the stake; if great scientific discoveries are to be established, men like Galileo, Galvani, Faraday and Edison must spend sleepless nights and laborious days through long years. If great religious truths are to be enunciated as the priceless heirloom of pilgrim souls, men like Baxter, Bunyan or Charles Simeon must be willing to undergo ostracism, misrepresentation and contempt. Before Samuel could be given to his people, Hannah must be a woman of a sorrowful spirit.

Some few miles to the north of Jerusalem, on the confines of the territories of Ephraim and Benjamin, was situated the town of Ramathaim-zophim. It was also known as Ramah, and has passed into New Testament history as Arimathea, the town from which came the man who begged of Pilate the body of the Lord. Ramathaim means the two Ramahs, as there were probably an upper and a lower city, to which reference is made later in the story (1 Sam. 9:13). Zophim recalls the name of an ancestor of Elkanah named Zuph, who appears to have been a man of considerable importance and to have given his name to the whole district (1 Chron. 6:35; 1 Sam. 9:5). In this mountain city a child was to be born who was to give it interest and importance not only during his lifetime, when it became the focus of the national life, but for centuries of years.

Towards the close of Samson's career in southern Judah there resided at Ramah a family consisting of Elkanah, a Levite, and his two wives, Hannah (Grace) and Peninnah (Pearl or Margaret). He had formerly lived in Ephraim, and was therefore considered to belong to that tribe (Joshua 21:20). That he had two wives was not a violation of the Levitical law, which did not forbid polygamy but carefully regulated the marriage law—penetrating the home-life with such ideals as would gradually bring men and women back to the original institution of Paradise (Mark 10:4–9).

It is supposed that Elkanah brought a second wife into his home because of Hannah's childlessness; but, whatever had been the cause, the step had been fraught with misery. The house at Ramah was filled with bickering and strife, which was augmented as child after child fell to the lot of Peninnah while Hannah was still childless. Apart from all else, her desolate condition was an almost intolerable condition (Gen. 30:1); but that it should be made the subject of biting sarcasm and bitter taunts was the occasion of the most poignant grief. The pain was not confined to Ramah, but seems to have reached its climax when, according to the Hebrew custom, the household went up to offer unto the Lord the yearly sacrifice, and Hannah was compelled to witness the many portions which fell to the lot of her rival because of all her sons and daughters when, at the sacrificial feast, after offering to Jehovah the victims they had brought, they retired to feast on the remainder. Then it was that the needy sat upon the dunghill and the poor in the dust; then it was that her soul was pierced as by the sword of the Lord and drew near unto the grave; then it was that the hunger of her soul could not be appeased even by the consciousness of Elkanah's fond affection (1:5, 8; 2:5–8). But out of this soul-travail the joy of her life and the savior of her country was to be born.

2

A WOMAN'S ANGUISH OF HEART

(1 Samuel 1:15)

"Unanswered yet? Faith cannot be unanswered,
Her feet were firmly planted on the Rock;
Amid the wildest storms she stands undaunted,
Nor quails before the loudest thundershock.
She knows Omnipotence has heard her prayer,
And cries 'It shall be done' sometime, somewhere."

BROWNING

WE MAY infer that Hannah's barrenness and the provocation of her rival were not the only reasons for Hannah's sorrow. As her noble song proves, she was saturated with the most splendid traditions and hopes of her people; her soul was thrilling with the conceptions that inspired the songs of Moses. Stricken with an agony of grief for the anarchy and confusion around her, she longed with passionate desire to enshrine her noblest self in a child who perhaps should resuscitate the ebbing prosperity of the nation and set it on an enduring foundation. Frail woman that she was, she might not even hope to emulate a Jael or a Deborah, but she might save her people if she could only breathe her ardent nature into a child. Even if she were to be deprived of his presence and support from his earliest years, would she not be compensated a thousandfold if only the Lord would accept him as His own and use him to be the channel through which His redemptive schemes might be achieved? Levites ordinarily were consecrated to the Lord's service between the ages of thirty and fifty, but her son, if only she might have a man child, would be given to the Lord all the days of his life, and no razor would ever come upon his flowing locks.

On one occasion, while the feast was proceeding at Shiloh, it seemed as though Hannah could restrain herself no longer, and after her people had eaten and drunk—she fasting, save from tears—she rose up and returned to the outer court of the tabernacle. Most of its ancient glory had departed. Probably only a few curtains were draped around the ark and the other sacred furniture which had escaped the wreck of the previous two or three hundred years; and this simple structure was, if we may credit Rabbinical tradition, surrounded by a low stone wall, at the gate of which was a seat or throne for the high priest. "And she was in bitterness of soul, and prayed unto the Lord, and wept sore." Others went with burnt offerings, but she with the broken heart which God will not despise. She didn't chide God, but she held out her cup of trial, that it might become a cup of salvation.

We are told that "she prayed," and it becomes us to study her prayer and its issue.

It was heart-prayer. It is the custom of Easterners to pray audibly, but as she stood beside Eli's seat (v. 26) she spoke in her heart; her lips moved, but her voice was not heard. This indicates that she had made many advances in the divine life and had come to know the secret of heart-fellowship with God. Hers were not vain repetitions, but such an interchange of spirit with spirit, of need with supply, of hunger with satisfaction, of the human with the divine, as requires no speech, for speech could not convey those "groanings which cannot be uttered."

It was based on a new name for God. She appealed to Jehovah under a new title, "Jehovah of hosts," as though it was nothing to

Him to summon into existence an infant spirit whom she might call child. She asked Him to look down from the myriads of holy spirits who circled round His throne and did His behests, to her dire affliction and anguish. She vowed in words which Elkanah by his silence or consent afterwards ratified (Num. 30:6–15) that she did not want this inestimable boon for herself merely but for the kingdom and glory of God, and that her son would be a Nazarite from his birth, abstaining from intoxicating drink, his locks unshorn, his body undefiled by contact with the dead (Num. 6:1–12).

It was definite prayer. "Give unto thine handmaid a man child." "For this child I prayed." So many of our prayers miscarry because they are aimed at no special goal. We launch them aimlessly in the air, and wonder that they achieve nothing. How many of God's professing children would be nonplussed if, on leaving God's audience chamber on any morning, they were questioned as to what precious gift they had gone thither to obtain. We are too often contented with asking generally that God would bless those with whom we are connected, without entering specifically into the case of any. Experienced saints who are versed in the art of intercessory prayer tell us of the marvelous results which have accrued when they have set themselves to pray definitely for the salvation of individuals, or for some good and perfect gift on their behalf.

There is a notable instance of this in the life of Bishop Hannington of Uganda. It is recorded in the diary of a fellow clergyman who had known him at the university, that on a certain day he was led to pray definitely for his friend; and almost simultaneously Hannington notes in *his* diary that he was conscious of unusual drawings towards God.

It was prayer without reserve. "I have poured out my soul before the Lord." Ah, how good it would be if we could more often follow Hannah's example! We pour out our secrets to confidential friends and in many instances have reason bitterly to repent; or, if we commit our cause to God, we tell Him one side of the case—our side—and hide from Him the other. Often the matter would be ended if we dared to pour out all our soul—not defending ourselves, not apologizing, not glossing over what demanded clear and unequivocal confession. When the heart is breaking, when its frail machinery seems unable to sustain the weight of its anxiety, when its cords are strained to the point of snapping, then, as you remember these things, pour out the depths of your soul (Ps. 42:4).

It was persevering prayer. "It came to pass, as she *continued* praying before the Lord." Not that either she or we can claim to be heard for our much speaking, but when the Lord lays some burden on us we cannot do other than wait before Him.

It was prayer that received its coveted boon. Eli was seated in his place at the entrance to the sanctuary. His notice was attracted by Hannah, though she was indifferent to all around. At first his attention was probably arrested by the signs of her excessive sorrow, and he expected that she would pour out her prayers in an audible voice, as so many other burdened souls were likely to do. But since her lips moved, while her voice was not heard, the high priest thought she was drunk, and rather rudely and coarsely broke in on her with the rebuke, "How long wilt thou be drunken? Put away thy wine from thee." Therein another proof was given of the inability of the priesthood to understand and sympathize with the best spirit and temper of the time. Eli judged after the sight of his eyes, and clearly the mind of God had not been revealed to him. He had degenerated into the mere official, from whom the divine purposes were concealed.

Hannah answered the unjust reproach with great meekness. "No," she said, "it isn't as you think. I have drunk neither wine nor strong drink, but have poured out my spirit unto the Lord." She had already suffered so much that this last misapprehension could not seriously add to her burden. She was content to cast it, with all the rest, on God; and she realized, even before Eli replied, that the merciful Burden-bearer had heard and answered her prayer. She had entered into the spirit of the prayer, which not only asks, but takes. She anticipated those wonderful words which, more than any others, disclose the secret of prevailing supplication: "All things whatsoever ye pray and ask for, believe that ye have received them, and ye shall have them" (Mark 11:24). Even before the words of Eli, "Go in peace, and the God of Israel grant thy petition that thou hast asked of Him," had fallen like a summer shower on a parched land, she knew that she had prevailed, and the peace of God, which passeth all understanding, filled and kept her mind and heart. And she said, "Let thy servant find grace in thy sight." So she went her way and ate, and her face was no longer sad. Well may Anstice sing:

> *"Could we but kneel, and cast our load,*
> *E'en while we pray, upon our God,*
> *Then rise with lightened cheer."*

Too often we return from prayer with sad faces and burdened hearts. We have not cast our burden on the Lord, or if we have done so we have taken it back again. There has been no interchange and no exchange. We have failed to abandon our weights, anxieties and sins, leaving them in the hands of our Almighty Friend, receiving instead beauty for ashes, the oil of joy for mourning and the garment of praise for the spirit of heaviness.

The next day was fixed for their return home. "And they rose up in the morning early, and worshiped before the Lord, and returned, and came to their house in Ramah." But what an altered woman she was! How differently she has borne herself in that last brief visit to the holy shrine! And with what a glad face she entered the home which had been associated with such sorrow. Peninnah must have wondered what had happened to make so great a change; but Elkanah was the confidant of her secret, and his faith was made stronger by her unquestioning trust (v. 23)

The Workings of Sorrow.—In this prayer we can trace the harvest sown in years of suffering. Only one who had greatly suffered could have poured out such a prayer. The notes of resignation, of chastened submission to the will of God, of appeal as from the dust, of the abandonment of all hope save in God, of the simple desire for His kingdom and righteousness, are touched with infinite delicacy and tenderness by this sorrowful woman's hand. Sorrow gives an indefinable beauty to the soul. The blue of heaven does not seem so beautiful in rainless Egypt as in countries where the atmosphere is saturated with moisture. "What do you think of her singing?" asked the trainer of a soprano vocalist. "She sings superbly," was his friend's reply, "but if I had anything to do with her training, I would need to break her heart." It may be that the long, sharp pain which has been your lot for these many years—the heart-hunger, the disappointed hopes, the silent waiting, the holding your peace, even from good—has been necessary to teach you how to pray, to lead you into the secret of a childlike faith, and to fit you to be the parent of some priceless gift to the world.

It fell out to Hannah according to her faith. Blessed was she that had believed, for there was a performance unto her of the promises which God had made to her secret soul. "The Lord remembered her, and it came to pass, when the time had come about, that she bare a son, and she called his name Samuel, saying, 'Because I have asked him of the Lord.'"

The good Elkanah had a new joy in his heart as he went up to offer unto the Lord his yearly sacrifice; and it would seem that he added to it some special expression of a vow that he had made—"the yearly sacrifice, *and his vow*." But Hannah abode at Ramah until the child was weaned, which would probably be on the completion of his third year, for at that age Levite children were permitted to be enrolled and to enter the house of the Lord (2 Chron. 31:16).

At last the time arrived when the child should be openly presented to the Lord. The parents set out on their solemn journey with their child. The mother's heart was now as full of praise as it had formerly been of sorrow. Her heart rejoiced in the Lord; her spirit was exalted in her God. The beggar was lifted from the dunghill to inherit the throne of glory. She had learned that there was no Rock like her God, and she rejoiced in His salvation. Her song, on which the Mother of our Lord modeled the Magnificat, is the outburst of a soul whose cup was simply overflowing with the lovingkindness of the Lord.

Presently the memorable journey from Ramah was finished. The sanctuary was again in sight, where she had suffered so poignantly and prayed so fervently. How it all rushed on her memory. "I am the woman that stood by thee here," she said to Eli. "For this child I prayed, and the Lord hath given me my petition."

Notice those words, "I stood by thee *here.*" How closely we associate certain experiences with certain spots. *Here* we suffered; *here* we resolved to live a new life; *here* we heard God speak. It was thus with Hannah. And was it not befitting that she should rejoice where she had sorrowed; that the harvest of joy should wave over the furrows where her tears had fallen so lavishly; that the blue skies should overarch the very spot where the dark clouds had lowered?

Take heart, O man or woman of a sorrowful spirit! Only suffer according to the will of God, and for no wrong or sinful cause! Suffer for His Church, for a lost world, for dying men! Travail in birth for souls! Exercise yourself faithfully for the coming of His kingdom! Bear the weight of some other soul, dear to you as life! And if you will await your Lord's time, He will bring you again to tread in garments of joy where you have stood in the drapery of woe. You shall come again from the land of the enemy. They that go forth and weep, bearing precious seed, shall doubtless, *doubtless,* DOUBTLESS come again, with rejoicing, bringing their sheaves with them.

3

THE YOUNG LEVITE

(1 Samuel 2 and 3)

"Be still! sad soul! lift thou no passionate cry,
But spread the desert of thy being bare
To the full searching of the All-seeing eye;
Wait!—and through dark misgiving, blank despair,
God will come down in pity, and fill the dry
Dead place with light, and life, and vernal air."

J. C. SHAIRP

DEAN STANLEY tells us that, in his gentler moments, Luther used to dwell on these early chapters of the books of Samuel with the tenderness which formed the occasional counterpoise to the ruder passions and enterprises of his stormy life. Indeed, students of the Scriptures in every age have been arrested by the figure of this little child girded with his linen ephod, or in the little robe which his mother brought him from year to year, when she came up with her husband to offer the yearly sacrifice.

With what passionate and almost irrepressible desire the mother must have anticipated that annual visit, all too transient to satisfy her natural longings. It must have been hard enough to leave him at all at so tender an age as three; and specially with the women who seem to have been regularly occupied in the service of the tabernacle and to whose care he was probably entrusted. Probably, however, not all of them were infected with the shameful sin into which several seem to have been seduced (1 Sam. 2:22, R.V.). There may have been among them some like Anna the prophetess, who departed not from the sacred shrine, worshiping with fastings and supplications, night and day (Luke 2:37). These would attend to the physical needs of the child, while his training in the law and the elements of such education as was possible would be under the direct supervision of the high priest.

But Hannah was solaced for her deprivation. There was the precious memory of those early years when he had filled the house with his childish prattle and she had been able to sow in the receptive soil of his tender heart the seeds of manhood's harvest. Other children, also, were born to her; and, as three sons and two daughters grew up at her knees, surely the thought of their little brother, in his sacred office a continual inspiration, must have been a subject of lively and perennial interest. We need not accept the Jewish legend which narrates that, as one of Hannah's children was born, one of Peninnah's died. Such an infliction would have given no satisfaction to Hannah and have been unkind to Elkanah. It was enough that Jehovah had vindicated the woman's wrongs, as He will assuredly vindicate all those who when they are reviled revile not again, when they suffer threaten not, but commit themselves and their complaint to Him who judgeth righteously. Peaceful, reverent and loving thoughts filled the mother's heart as she worked on the little robe, which in shape was of the pattern which, probably, Mary made for her Son: "woven in one piece from the top and without seam," which the soldiers would not tear.

The Influence of a Mother.—Mothers still make garments for their children—not on the loom or with their busy needles merely, but by their holy and ennobling characters displayed from day to day before young and quickly observant eyes, by their words and conversation, and by the habits of their daily devotion. What the children see they imitate, and unconsciously array themselves in the gentleness or rudeness, the reverence for religion or indifference, the refinement or coarseness of manner, which are daily presented to their gaze. As fish take on the mottled color of the ground on which they lie, and as the plovers change their plumage to match the winter or the spring, so children wear the robes which their mother's character and behavior, temper and tones, weave for them.

"And so the child did minister unto the Lord before Eli the priest": slept his innocent sleep unconscious of the sins around him, attracted the growing attachment of the old man by his reverent affection and endearing ways, and gave many evidences that he was being prepared to become a link between God and His people, a mediator between the old and the new—between the turbulent days of Samson and the splendid peace of the reign of Solomon.

NOTICE THE SACRILEGE AND SINS OF ELI'S SONS. "Now the sons of Eli were sons of Belial [*worthlessness*]; they knew not the Lord, nor the due of the priests from the people" (2:12, R.V. margin). The law of Moses authorized the priest to take as his portion, instead of fees in coin, the whole of the sin offerings, and the breast and right shoulder of the peace offerings—the fat only of the latter being burned on the altar, while the remainder of the animal was handed back to the offerer, to be consumed by himself, his sons and his daughters, his menservants and his maidservants, and the Levite that was within his gates (Deut. 12:12). It was befitting, as the apostle states it, that those who ministered about sacred things should eat of the things of the temple, and that those who waited upon the altar should have their portion with the altar (1 Cor. 9:13).

The first act of every peace offering was the sprinkling of blood upon the altar round about; the second was the burning of the internal fat. It was never eaten, but always consumed by fire. The flame fed on it as the food of God, who, so to speak, ate with the accepted worshiper (Lev. 3:16–17). After this solemn rite was performed, the priest's portion was waved and presented to God, and the group of worshipers made way for others, carrying away with them their portion for the joyful sacrificial feast.

Here Eli's sons stepped in with their rapacious greed. Not satisfied with their legally allotted portion, they sent their servant after the retiring group with a three-pronged fork in his hand, and while the meat was boiling for the sacred meal he thrust his trident into the cauldron and claimed as the priest's perquisite whatever was brought up. "So they did in Shiloh unto all the Israelites that came thither."

But even this did not long satisfy them. They went on to insist that after the breast and shoulder had been handed them, but before the remainder had been put to boil, they should be supplied with raw meat from the offerer's portion; nor would they burn the fat—which was the essential part of the whole sacrifice, and one for which the worshipers must needs wait—until their demands were satisfied. This final touch seems to have aroused the long-suffering people to exasperation. "At least," they said, "wait till the Lord's portion has been presented before you proceed to your lawless depredations. Burn the fat, and then take as much as you will." "No," was the ruthless answer of the priest, "but you shall give it to me now or I will take what I choose by force." "And the sin of the young men was very great before the Lord, for men abhorred the offering of the Lord."

It becomes us to inquire with much anxiety and heart-searching whether we, as the servants of Christ, are doing or abetting things which cause men to abhor that holy Name by which we are called. We may begin with our own characters and habits, and thence proceed to our doctrinal statements and ecclesiastical arrangements. Rightly or wrongly, I have heard of men forswearing the Christian religion to which they were once attached because professing Christians were so dilatory in paying their debts, so evasive in their excuses, so profuse in promises that were never kept, so difficult to please, so thoughtless and careless in their demands on co-workers and servants, so touchy and fretful, so liable to do things in business which high-minded men of the world would not permit. I have heard of men, rightly or wrongly, turning from misstatements of Christian doctrine which revolted their moral sense and made God our Father as cruel as Chemosh or Molech. I have heard of men, rightly or wrongly, refusing to enter places of worship because of the class distinctions which were maintained and the strong dislike with which a stranger's admission into the family pew was resented. For these things too many excuse their refusal of the gospel and their absence from the house of prayer.

Not content with their extortionate greed, Hophni and Phinehas perpetrated the vilest excesses of heathenism amid the woods and vineyards of Shiloh. Licentious rites had from time immemorial been associated with heathen festivals, but never before had they sullied the sacred vestures of the priests of Aaron's line. So abandoned were these young men, though they had wives of their own, that they did not scruple to lead astray the women who were appointed to perform the various offices about the sanctuary that demanded female labor.

Remonstrances were addressed to the aged priest; he heard of their evil doings from all the people (2:23), but instead of strong disapproval and stringent threats he contented himself with a mild rebuke. He said unto them, "Why do ye these things? Nay, my sons! For it is no good report that I hear. Ye make the Lord's people transgress." On this the Divine Judge makes the terrible comment that Eli's sons made themselves vile, and he restrained them not. He had reproved but not restrained them. Even supposing they had disregarded the reproof of their father, they could hardly have defied a dismissal insisted on by him as high priest, embodying as he did the highest authority in the realm. And for this weak laxity he was condemned and deposed. A man of God declared to them: "Thus says the Lord: 'Why do you kick at My sacrifice and My offering?' Therefore the Lord, the God of Israel, says: 'I said indeed that thy house and the house of thy father would walk before Me forever'; but now the Lord says, 'Far be it from Me, for those who honor Me I will honor, and those who despise Me shall be lightly esteemed.'"

The Need of Family Training.—This suggests a very serious inquiry for those who take a prominent position in the church and before the world, but who neglect their own families. We are held responsible for our children. Our weakness in restraining them is sin, which will be inevitably followed not only by their punishment but by our own. Better do less in the church and the world than allow your children to grow up a misery to themselves and a reproach to you. Remember that one essential qualification for office in the early Church was the wise and wholesome rule of house and children. If a man could not keep his children in submission with proper respect and rule his house well, he surely could not know how to take care of the house of God (1 Tim. 3:4, 12). Probably Eli had not begun early enough. The wise parent will begin training children from their earliest months, to say nothing of years; and the early strain of careful observation and chastisement may well be lightened and eased by remembering that the child who from the earliest is trained in God's way will not depart from it when he is old.

Above all, let us seek the conversion of our young children to God. The apostle distinctly affirms that God will give us life for those who sin *not unto death* (1 John 5:16); and this description is, above all, applicable to little children. Surely He will not be unrighteous to forget the tears and prayers, or to overlook the faith, of those who travail a second time till Christ is formed in the hearts of their offspring. Hear my testimony: I, as the child of godly parents, who cannot date the hour of my conversion because the love of God stole over my heart in early boyhood like the dawn of a summer sky, put my seal to this word of God as true: "My Spirit that is upon thee, and my words which I have put in thy mouth, shall not depart out of thy mouth, nor out of the mouth of thy seed, nor out of the mouth of thy seed's seed, from henceforth and forever" (Isa. 59:21).

4

THE VISION OF GOD

(1 Samuel 3)

"Oh! give me Samuel's mind,
  A sweet, unmurmuring faith,
Obedient and resigned
  To Thee in life and death;
That I may read with childlike eyes
Truths that are hidden from the wise."

J. D. BURNS

IT IS very touching to notice the various references to the child Samuel as they recur during the progress of the narrative, especially those in which an evident contrast is intended between his gentle innocence and the wild license of Eli's sons—it is like a peal of sweet bells ringing on amid the crash of a storm.

Hannah said, "I will bring him, *that he may appear before the Lord, and there abide forever.*" "And she . . . brought him unto the house of the Lord in Shiloh; *and the child was young.*" "'As long as he liveth he is lent to the Lord.' *And he worshiped the Lord there.*" "*And the child did minister unto the Lord* before Eli the priest." "Now the sons of Eli were wicked men; they knew not the Lord: . . . and the sin of the young men was very great before the Lord, for men abhorred the offering of the Lord, *but Samuel ministered before the Lord, being a child.*" "Now Eli was very old, and he heard all that his sons did unto all

Israel. . . . Notwithstanding they hearkened not unto the voice of their father, because the Lord would slay them. *And the child Samuel grew on, and was in favor with the Lord, and also with men.*" "And there came a man of God unto Eli, and said unto him, . . .'Wherefore kick ye at my sacrifice and at mine offering?'. . . *And the child Samuel ministered unto the Lord before Eli.*" "And the Lord said, 'Behold, I will do a thing in Israel, at which both the ears of everyone that heareth it shall tingle.'. . . *And Samuel grew, and the Lord was with him, and did let none of his words fall to the ground; and all Israel from Dan even to Beer-sheba knew that Samuel was established to be a prophet of the Lord.*" "The Lord revealed Himself to Samuel in Shiloh, by the word of the Lord, *and the word of Samuel came to all Israel.*"

His life seems to have been one unbroken record of blameless purity, integrity and righteousness. One purpose ran through all his years, threading them together in an unbroken series. There were no gaps nor breaks; no lapses into sensuality or selfishness; no lawless deeds in that wild, lawless age. Towards the end of a long life he was able to appeal to the verdict of the people in memorable words which attested his consciousness of unsullied rectitude: "I am old and gray-headed, . . . and *I have walked before you from my youth unto this day.* Here I am; witness against me before the Lord and before His anointed: Whose ox have I taken, or whose ass have I taken, or whom have I defrauded? Whom have I oppressed, or of whose hand have I received any bribe?" And they said, "Thou hast not defrauded us, nor oppressed us, neither hast thou taken aught of any man's hand."

It was a beautiful life—strong in its faculty of administration, wise in steering the nation from the rule of the judges into the royal state of the kings, unimpeachably just, but blamelessly pure— towering above his contemporaries like a peak of glistening chryso- lite on which the sunlight plays while all the valleys beneath are wrapped in scudding clouds and sweeping rain.

Samuel was not a prophet in the sense of foretelling the long future and was not possessed of Isaiah's genius and eloquence; his only contribution to his age was a saintly character, which reminds us of that of James, the brother of our Lord, whose pure white robe was emblematic of his spotless character. Samuel was the James of the Old Testament; and it was by his saintliness, the moral grandeur of his character, that he arrested the ruin of his people.

We too may be called to face an era of change; our eyes may have to witness the passing of the old and the coming of the new. It may be that in our time the Lord will shake once more, not earth only, but heaven, that the things which cannot be shaken may remain; in our time also ancient landmarks may be removed, as familiar and sacred as the tabernacle of Shiloh and the ark of the covenant to Israel. But there is one property within our reach which need never pass away, which shall remain unimpaired and radiant through the years—and that is unblemished character, a soul stainlessly arrayed, and the holy life in which these shall be embodied. "Let Thy work appear unto Thy servants, and Thy glory unto their children. And let the beauty of the Lord our God be upon us, and establish Thou the work of our hands upon us; yea, the work of our hands, establish Thou it."

The noblest gift that any of us can make to our fatherland or age is an undefiled character and a stainless life. Let us live our best in the power of the Spirit of God and prove that the God of Pentecost is living still.

I. THE TRANSITION OF A YOUNG SOUL.—For Samuel, however, a great change was necessary and imminent. Up to this moment he had lived largely in the energy and motive-power of his mother's intense religious life. It was needful that he should EXCHANGE THE TRADITIONAL FOR THE EXPERIENTIAL. His faith must rest, not on the assertions of another's testimony, but because for himself he had seen, and tasted, and handled the Word of Life. Not at second hand, but at first, the word of the Lord must come to him, and be passed on to all Israel. Probably this change comes to everyone who desires and seeks after the best and richest life. You may be the child of a pious home, where from boyhood or girlhood you were trained in the traditions of evangelical religion: you were expected to pray and to serve God. You have been borne along by a blessed momentum. But suppose for a minute that that momentum should fail you; have you come to apprehend Christ as a living Reality for yourself? It may be that God, out of mercy to you, will break up and destroy the traditions and forms on which you have been relying, so that the eternal and divine may stand forth apparent to your spiritual perception and be apprehended by yourself for yourself, as though they were meant for you alone. It is a great hour in the history of the soul when the traditional, to which it has become habituated by long habit and use, is suddenly exchanged for the open vision of God—when we say with Job, "I have heard of Thee with the hearing of the ear, but now mine eye seeth Thee"; when we say with the apostle, "Leaving the things that are behind, and reaching forth to those that are before, I press toward the mark."

Will you believe then that God may be coming very near you and is about to reveal Himself to you in the Lord Jesus, as He will not do unto the world? He is about to transform your life and lift it to an altogether new level, so that though you may have to face the old circumstances it shall be from a higher standpoint—even as the spiral staircase is always returning to the same viewpoint though always at the elevation of some few additional feet.

II. THE VISION OF THE YOUNG EYES.—(1) When God came near His young servant, it seemed as though *He placed His seal upon his faithfulness.* Hitherto but small services had been required of him. To close and open the doors of the tabernacle; to light the seven-branched lampstand in the late afternoon, and supply it with pure olive oil every morning; to render little services to the aged priest, whether by day or night—such were the duties assigned to him and performed with punctilious care. It was fitting that he who had shown himself faithful in a very little should have a larger and wider sphere assigned to him.

(2) *The vision* came as night was beginning to yield to dawn; but "the lamp had not yet gone out in the temple of the Lord, where the ark of God was." Thrice the boy was startled from his innocent slumbers on his little bed in the chamber he occupied adjacent to the sacred building. He heard his name called softly, tenderly, lovingly, and was convinced that Eli needed him, and thrice sped across the intervening space to report himself. Once, and again, and yet again, he ran unto Eli, and said, "Here am I, for thou calledst me."

When God approaches us to reveal His Son in us, the tendency is always to speed with all haste to some place, or some spiritual adviser, where we suppose that the interpretation of the vision will be given. Young converts, for instance, are apt to say, "If only I could have my questions answered by such a man of God, I am sure I would get a blessing," and thus they are kept in constant perturbation, running backwards and forwards, repeating Samuel's vain experience—running to Eli and saying, "Surely you called me, and can interpret for me the vision and the voice."

(3) *Eli was very wise in his treatment of the lad.* He might have posed as the sole depository of the divine secrets, might have warned the lad against listening to vain delusions, might have given way to ungoverned jealousy and suspicion, might have stood on the dignity and pride of office. But instead of any of these, without the slightest trace of hurt pride, he took the boy's hand in his and, so to speak, led him into the Divine Presence, knowing full well that the seals of sacred office, which had been taken from himself, were about to be laid on those youthful palms.

If Eli had inherited merely the traditions of the priesthood, he would have stood between that young soul and God, hearing its confession, wielding over it a terrorizing influence and directing it, as acting in the place of God. Instead of this, however, the old man said sweetly, "Go and lie down again, and it shall be when He shall call thee, that thou shalt say, 'Speak, Lord, for Thy servant heareth.'"

It is not the business of the Christian minister to lord it over the eager and aroused disciple, to demand confession or offer absolution. He ought rather to say in effect: "You need more than we can give. God, and God only, can satisfy you. Go, and lie down again. Be quiet. Let your soul be still before God. Wait, for He will assuredly come again. And it shall be, if He calls you, that you shall say, 'Speak, Lord, for Thy servant heareth.'"

As Thomas à Kempis puts it:

> "Speak, Lord, for Thy servant heareth."
> Let not Moses speak unto me, nor any of the prophets, but rather do Thou speak, O Lord God, the Inspirer and Enlightener of all the prophets; for Thou alone without them canst perfectly instruct me, but they without Thee can profit nothing.
>
> Speak Thou unto me, to the comfort, however imperfect, of my soul, and to the amendment of my whole life, and to Thy praise, and glory, and honor everlasting.

(4) *The message entrusted to the lad was a very terrible one.* We cannot wonder that he feared to tell Eli the vision. With *a beautiful modesty and reticence* he set about the duties of the day, and opened, as usual, the doors of the house of the Lord. It was not for him to blurt out the full thunder which had burst on him. This was another lovely trait in the boy's character. But he had misread Eli's character; he did not realize that men like him will die but not murmur—will resign themselves without a word of expostulation

or defense, determined to know the worst, and when they know it will meekly answer, "It is the Lord; let Him do what seemeth Him good."

(5) *It is well to notice that the Lord revealed Himself to Samuel in Shiloh "by the word of the Lord."* Let us not seek for revelations through dreams or visions, but by the word of God. Nothing is more harmful than to contract the habit of listening for voices, and sleeping in order to dream. All manner of vagaries come in by that door. It is best to take in hand and read the Scriptures reverently, carefully, thoughtfully—crying, "Speak, Lord, for Thy servant heareth." And in response there will come one clear, defined and repeated message, asseverated and accentuated with growing distinctness from every part of the inspired volume. "This is the way—walk in it; this is My will—do it; this is My word—speak it." Let us hear what God the Lord shall speak.

5

MISFORTUNE ON MISFORTUNE

(1 Samuel 4–6)

"Oh, the outward hath gone! but in glory and power
The Spirit surviveth the things of an hour;
Unchanged, undecaying, its Pentecost flame
On the heart's secret altar is burning the same."

WHITTIER

THE scanty records of these chapters (4:1–7:17) bridge over a considerable tract of Scripture, covering, perhaps, forty years. The details of Samuel's life and growing influence given by the sacred historian during that period are very fragmentary. But the narrative of events is interesting and must be understood by those who would have a right conception of the great service that Samuel rendered to his people. It will appear, also, that there is a remarkable parallel, not only between those days of anarchy and our own, but between the work he did and the work that is needed as urgently in the present day.

It was an age of disunion and anarchy. After the deaths of Joshua, Caleb, and of all that generation, "there arose another generation after them, which knew not the Lord, nor yet the work which He had wrought for Israel" (Judges 2:10). There was no man, and no tribe, able to unite the people under one leadership, or to recall them to the lofty monotheism—the worship of the one Jehovah—which characterized the founder of their common-wealth. The bonds of their national unity were loosened; each tribe and each great city asserted its independence of all the rest. The heart of the national life beat feebly, and, to quote again the expressive phrase which so completely represents the age of the judges, "Every man did what was right in his own eyes."

The only common center was afforded by the tabernacle, the ark, and the high priesthood; but even the influence of these had become greatly reduced, for "the children of Israel forsook Jehovah, the God of their fathers, which brought them up out of the land of Egypt, and followed other gods, the gods of the peoples that were round about them, and bowed themselves down unto them."

There was, therefore, nothing to hinder the steady encroachments of the neighboring nations. Now it was the children of Ammon on the east, then the Amalekites and Midianites from the desert, and again the Philistines on the southwest, that broke in on the land of Promise. From time to time judges were raised up, but their authority was only temporary and limited. For the most part it ceased with their death, and was the means of delivering only a section of the land. "When the Lord raised them up judges, then the Lord was with the judge, and saved them out of the hand of their enemies all the days of the judge, . . . but it came to pass, when the judge was dead, that they turned back, and dealt more corruptly than their fathers" (Judges 2:18–19).

Our story is specially connected with the southern and midland districts of Canaan, which, notwithstanding Samson's heroic exploits—for he was contemporary with Samuel's early years—lay under the tyrannous yoke of the Philistines, who seem about this time to have been largely reinforced from the original seat of their empire on the neighboring island of Crete, and to have made the position of the Hebrews almost intolerable.

In these Philistines stealing up from their own territories and cities to dominate the Hebrews, in the land which God gave them for a heritage—a land to which the Philistines could have no possible claim, but which was certainly the allotted possession of the chosen people—I see the type of much which is always taking place in our own experience. For instance, they stand for unholy desires and evil habits from which we were once set free by the risen Son of God, but which, in subsequent years, may have come back to assert their former sway and tyranny. And again, they represent the inroads of worldliness into the Church and of wickedness into the State. The forces of evil are never at rest. Just as the spirit of destruction and waste is perpetually at work in untiling our roofs, stripping off our wallpapers, pulling down our walls, and sowing our gardens with weeds while we sleep, so the evil tendencies in the heart, the Church and the nation are ever warring against the law of the mind and bringing men into captivity to the law of sin.

In the insidious attempts to rob us of our Rest Day and to turn it into one of public amusement; in the unblushing effrontery of vice in various forms; in the threatened domination of all other interests by the mad greed for money; in the spirit of amusement which infects society; in the worldliness and luxury which divide with the spiritual and heavenly the hearts and lives of professing Christians—we are brought face to face with the bands of the Philistines as they steal up from their lowlands to the uplands of religious constancy and strength. They have no rights, but they never fail to assert their pretensions; and sometimes we almost lose heart and begin to question whether there is any use in opposing them.

Why this constant strife? Were it not better to yield the point in controversy and to acquiesce?

At other times, like the children of Israel, we are goaded to make one desperate effort for freedom.

I. An Ill-fated Attempt.—"Now Israel went out against the Philistines to battle, and pitched beside Ebenezer, and the Philistines pitched in Aphek" ("the Fortress," perhaps in the neighborhood of Bethlehem). From these words we infer that the war was started by Israel throwing down the gage of battle because the yoke of Philistia was too galling to be endured; but it is almost certain that from the first it was an ill-starred and badly managed campaign.

Very distinct directions were issued by Moses as to the way in which a campaign should be commenced and conducted (Deut. 20), but none of them seems to have been put in force on this occasion. No priest was called in to ask counsel of God, or bless the going forth of the Israelite hosts. Not even Samuel, whom the people were beginning to recognize as the servant and prophet of Jehovah, seems to have been consulted. It was the sudden flaming out of a spirit of hatred and revenge from a race of slaves who were stung to the quick by the taunts, the insults and the scorpion-whips of their masters.

Such has been the spirit in which we have sometimes turned against the powerful sins which have asserted their mastery over us. We have seen the ruin to which they were bringing us, we have winced at the shame and indignation which they were causing to others, we have felt insulted and outraged in any lingering sense of honor and nobility that may have escaped the general wreck, and we have turned against our tormentors. We have signed the pledge against the use of intoxicants, we have taken a solemn oath nevermore to yield to our besetting sin, we have vowed that we will be free. But within a month we have been back in the old state. It has not gone better with us than with Israel, for this battle is not to the strong, nor this race to the swift.

It went hard with the Israelites. Their hosts, hastily summoned and insufficiently armed, suffered a heavy defeat. Four thousand men lay dead on the battlefield, and a spirit of intimidation and dismay spread through the entire host. Such will ever be the result when God's people leave Him out of account. Their education is so costly and necessary that He can afford to let them suffer, again and again, that an arrest may be put on courses that are not good.

II. The Ark, but Not God, to the Rescue.—On the evening of that disastrous day the elders of Israel held a council of war (4: 3). It was evident that their defeat must be attributed to some failure in their relations with Jehovah. They said, "Why hath *the Lord* smitten us today before the Philistines?" They were conscious that they had left Him out of their reckoning, and suddenly they thought of a happy expedient by which they might almost compel Him to enter into the fray and take sides with them against their foes. "Let us fetch," they cried, "the ark of the covenant of the Lord out of Shiloh, that it may come among us, and save us out of the hand of our enemies."

They remembered the wonderful scenes in which that ark had played a part—how the waters of the Jordan had fled before it, and the walls of Jericho had fallen down. Its going forth (in the words of their great lawgiver) had always meant the scattering and flight of Jehovah's foes. Surely it would do the same again. They did not realize that God's very present help depended not on the presence of a material symbol but on moral and spiritual conditions which they should have set themselves to understand and fulfill. It was much as though a high Sacramentarian should depend for deliverance from trial by wearing some amulet or charm, or even carrying a piece of the consecrated wafer in a golden casket upon his person, instead of exercising himself in manly faith and prayer.

The arrival of the ark, in due course, borne by the Levites, and accompanied by the sons of Eli as its custodians, was received with the exultant shouts of the entire host. Eli had evidently been most unwilling to allow it to leave the sacred enclosure—"his heart trembled for the ark of God"—but he had yielded too often and too long to be able to sustain a successful protest; and probably no one else had any misgivings, for "when the ark of the covenant of the Lord came into the camp, all Israel shouted with a great shout, so that the earth rang again."

As soon as the Philistines, by means of their scouts, were acquainted with the cause of this exuberant outburst, they were correspondingly depressed, for they, too, identified the presence of the God of Israel with the advent of the ark, which had always been associated in their minds with the hand of "these mighty gods that smote the Egyptians with plagues in the wilderness." Neither had they any idea of those moral considerations on which alone the cooperation of God could be given. "Woe unto us!" they cried, "for there hath not been such a thing heretofore. Woe unto us! Who shall deliver us?"

It was necessary that a decisive answer should be given to these materialistic conceptions of the Hebrews and their foes. It must be demonstrated that the mere possession of the symbol of the Covenant was valueless so long as the strange gods and the Ashtaroth were tenaciously cherished, and the abominations of the heathen were constantly and shamelessly pursued (7:3–4). The asseveration of holy words, the quoting of venerable precedents, the reliance on sacred emblems are alike in vain, unless the heart is pure and the hands clean. "If I regard iniquity in my heart, the Lord will not hear me."

The Philistines seem to have stirred themselves to deeds of desperate valor because they believed that they were to fight not only against flesh and blood, but against the deities who had led Israel in one long succession of victories. They advanced to the conflict with the words of their leaders ringing in their ears: "Be strong, and quit yourselves like men, O ye Philistines, that ye be not servants to the Hebrews, as they have been to you. Quit yourselves like men and fight" (see 1 Cor. 16:13).

The issue of that terrible day was disastrous in the extreme. "Israel was smitten, and they fled every man to his tent, and there was a very great slaughter, for there fell of Israel thirty thousand footmen." Around the ark the ground must have been heaped with corpses as the Hebrews fought desperately in defense of the symbol of their faith; but in vain, for the ark of God was taken, and the two sons of Eli were slain. Thus had Samuel foretold, and thus it befell.

That afternoon a Benjamite, with his clothes rent and dust upon his head, bore the tidings to the hamlets and villages that lay all along the ascending and open road to Shiloh, and, as he passed through eager and expectant groups, a wail arose that grew in volume as he sped onwards until it reached its climax in the city of the high priest—the capital, so far as there was any, of the entire land. "When the man came into the city, and told it, all the city cried out." On the still evening air arose a piercing outburst of lamentation, for what was there to hinder the immediate march of the victorious army on the defenseless city, deprived in one day of its warriors, and apparently of its God!

The old man, Eli, blind and anxious, had caused himself to be seated on his dais, facing on the main thoroughfare. He had a foreboding that bad news was in the air, and when the noise of the tumult arose he anxiously inquired of the attendant priests and Levites, and, perhaps, of Samuel, waiting as usual to respond to his least appeal for help, "What meaneth the noise of this tumult?" At the same moment the messenger appears to have burst into the presence of the little group, telling Eli who he was, and in answer to the eager inquiry of the high priest, "How went the matter, my son?" without warning or preface, and with no care to soften the asperity of the harsh words, he blurted out, with an ever-rising climax of dread awfulness: "Israel is fled before the Philistines, and there hath been also a great slaughter among the people, and thy two sons also, Hophni and Phinehas, are dead, and the ark of God is taken."

The old man received the tidings in silence. The three first shots hit him severely, but not mortally; but "when he made mention of the ark of God, he fell from off his seat backward by the side of the gate, and his neck brake and he died." With her last gasp the wife of Phinehas gathered up the horror of the situation with the single word "Ichabod,"which she uttered as the name of her child, prematurely born. It was sorrow indeed that she was a widow; sorrow that her father-in-law had died at the moment when he was needed so sorely; but sorrow most of all that the ark was taken, for with it the glory had departed. True soul that she was, she is worthy to be classed with Hannah in her loyal devotion to the name and house of God.

But worse troubles still befell. In frantic haste the Israelites bore away the remnants of the sacred tent and its furniture, and concealed them. In subsequent years they were at Nob (1 Sam. 21:1). The removal of these precious relics was hardly effected before the Philistine invasion burst on the deserted city as an overflowing flood. "Go ye now," says Jeremiah, in the Divine Name, "into My place which was in Shiloh, where I caused My name to dwell at the first, and see what I did to it for the wickedness of My people Israel" (Jer. 7:12). And the further fate of the city, which for 300 years had been the center of the national life and worship, may be guessed from the pathetic words of the Psalmist:

> *"He forsook the tabernacle of Shiloh,*
> *The tent which He pitched among men;*
> *And delivered His strength into captivity*
> *And His glory into the adversary's hand.*
> *He gave His people over also unto the sword,*
> *And was wroth with His inheritance.*
> *Fire devoured their young men,*
> *And their maidens were not praised in the marriage song;*
> *Their priests fell by the sword,*
> *And their widows made no lamentation."*
>
> (Ps. 78:60–64).

III. THE POWERFUL NAME OF GOD.—We need not concern ourselves to any great length with the most interesting adventures of
the ark, the sacred symbol of the worship of Jehovah. This part
of the history more closely concerns the growing illumination of
the surrounding nations as to the true nature of the God of Israel.

There was no better way by which the Spirit of God could
inform the people of Philistia as to His holiness and power than
that which He adopted in the present instance. They bore the ark
from the battlefield to the temple of Dagon in exuberant triumph.
It seemed as though they had not only triumphed over Israel but
over its tutelary deity, and that Dagon was superior to Jehovah.
But it would have been a great disaster had they been allowed to
cherish this idea in perpetuity. As in Egypt, centuries before, so
now in Philistia, God must reveal His unapproachable supremacy.
He cannot give His glory to another nor His praise to graven
images, and therefore He suits Himself to the crude and materialistic conceptions of these blinded idolaters and meets them in
their own sphere. They would not have been impressed by the
message of a prophet. They would have scouted and stoned anyone who opposed the universal national adoration of Dagon; but
they could not resist the conclusions forced on them when, on two
following mornings, they found his image prostrate before the emblem of Jehovah, and on the second occasion the head and arms
severed from the body so that the only part which was left intact
was the fish's tail with which the figure ended. That it might be
made still clearer that this was no coincidence but the act of God,
and that He had a controversy with them, a terrible plague of
"tumors" broke out on each successive city to which the ark was
removed, and a visitation of destructive vermin on the country
districts where it may have been deposited.

We must not suppose, of course, that God had no love towards
these untutored souls; but that there was no other way of con-

vincing them of His real nature and prerogatives. The plagues of Egypt were ordained not only to punish the sins of pride and obstinacy with which Pharaoh made himself strong against the Almighty, but that the Egyptians might be forced to recognize that He was the great God of heaven, of whom now and again they caught a glimpse. Similarly, in this instance, the prostrated form of Dagon, the painful disease by which they were smitten, and the devastation of their crops caused them to cry unto heaven (5:12), as though they realized that they were being dealt with by a greater than Dagon, by the great Being who was superior to all local gods. In after-years the Hebrew psalmists and prophets heaped scorn on the gods of the heathen that were no gods, and magnified Jehovah, who made the heavens; but the lesson took years to learn, and cost an infinite amount of pains and patience before monotheism became the generally admitted creed.

The reverence with which the Philistines refer to the God of Israel indicates that new and lofty conceptions were beginning to take the place of the low and materialistic ones that had degraded Jehovah to the level of their own local deities. "The cry of the city went up to heaven." "Ye shall give glory unto the God of Israel." "Take the ark of Jehovah."

What a sublime revelation this is of God's methods with man! With an infinite longing He desires to win the allegiance and devotion of all men. The consummate and unapproachable revelation which He has made for this purpose is in the Son of His love. "The only begotten of the Father, He hath declared Him." But of what use would it have been to speak of His Son in those early days when the hearts of men were darkened by the grossest conceptions and basest morals? No, line must be on line, precept upon precept! The times of ignorance must be "winked at." The light must be tempered to the weak and diseased eyes. God must adopt the language that could be understood by the children of men, whom He loved, just as in after-days our Lord exposed His hands and side to the incredulous Thomas, condescending to a method of demonstration which he could appreciate and had himself suggested. If the Philistines could have understood epistles like those of St. John they would, without doubt, have been written for their learning and correction, and communicated to them by some man of God; but since they could not understand such means of instruction, they were reached by the overthrow and shattering of their idol, the plagues which accompanied the progress of the ark, and the direction taken by the milk cows, who, while lowing for their little ones, bore their sacred burden along the straight road which led them from their home towards Beth-shemesh.

Similarly, the inhabitants of that Israelitish frontier town had to learn by a stern lesson that God was a holy God, and that He could not permit them to manifest a wanton curiosity and irreverence in handling the sacred emblem of His presence. To pry into the ark as they did, lifting its lid, and peering on its contents, was forbidden to the priests, and even the high priest himself—how much more to them! It had been distinctly asserted, when the two sons of Aaron perished on the day of their inauguration to the priesthood, that God would be sanctified in all that came nigh Him, and before all the people He would be glorified (Lev. 10:3).

The reverence due to Him must be shown to the vessels of the sanctuary, which were carefully veiled by the priests before they were taken up for transportation by the Levites (Num. 1:50–51; 4:5, 16–30). The swift retribution which followed on this act of irreverence extorted the reverent acknowledgment of the awful holiness of God, as the men of Beth-shemesh said, "Who is able to stand before this holy Lord God?" When, on the other hand, the ark had been reverently borne to Kirjath-jearim, the city of the woods, some three miles distant from the great valley of Beth-shemesh, on which the crops were goldening in the sun, and had been carefully entrusted to the custody of Abinadab and his son

Eleazar, the blessing that befell his house was an indication of the tender love and pity of the Divine nature, who is willing to dwell with him that is of a humble and lowly heart, and that trembleth at His word.

Oh, do not fear Jehovah with the dread of a craven heart, but with the loyal love and devotion of sons, and open your heart to receive not the ark of the covenant only, but Him whom God has set forth for a propitiation, and who is the propitiation for our sins, i.e., the mercy seat which covers the ark of the covenant, sprinkled with blood, and exactly fitting and hiding the tablets of the law beneath.

6

THE WORK OF RECONSTRUCTION

(1 Samuel 7:2)

"Be still and strong,
O Man, my Brother! Hold thy sobbing breath,
And keep thy soul's large window pure from wrong!
That so, as life's appointment issueth,
Thy vision may be clear to watch along
The sunset consummation—lights of death!"

E. B. BROWNING

WHILE the events described in the last chapter were in progress, Samuel was giving himself to the great and noble work of reconstruction. As soon as our flesh is lacerated, or our bones broken, Nature begins to pour out her reparative forces to renew the broken tissues, and so rebuild the ruined temple. As it is in physical life, so in spiritual there are always holy and gentle natures that are charged with the divine work of bridging over the roaring torrent of revolution, and of rearing new continents of order from the weltering ocean waste by which the previous land had been engulfed. Blessed work, indeed, is this, like the work of the Almighty, who, when the earth was without form and void, began to build in the midst of her the habitable places for man's existence.

To this Samuel devoted the twenty years that followed directly on the fatal field of Aphek. The Philistine invasion seems to have somewhat subsided from its first triumphant outburst, and to have retired from the occupancy of the interior portions of Israel. He was thus able to pursue his quiet and unobtrusive toils for his fatherland free from the zealous supervision and opposition to which, otherwise, he must have been subjected.

He seems to have taken up his abode in Ramah, so intimately associated with his earliest days. Here was his headquarters, where young men gathered to him and were formed into the earliest of the schools of the prophets, and where also he married and became the father of two sons. Their names are suggestive of their father's piety and walk with God, the name of the one being Joel—"Jehovah is God," and of the other Abiah—"Jehovah is my Father." Amid the general disturbance of the religious life in which he had been nurtured—with the ark in one place and the remnants of the tabernacle in another, with the discontinuance of the sacred rites and feasts which had been so great an assistance to piety in former years—Samuel nevertheless was able to walk with God and to preserve a devout religious life. Probably this is why God permits from time to time so great a shaking of the things that are made, that the things which cannot be shaken—the unseen and eternal—may be more clearly defined and more eagerly sought unto. In this present age, we have heard Him saying, "I will overturn, overturn, overturn"; we have seen theories of inspiration rudely assailed, churches menaced with destruction, ancient creeds ruthlessly questioned; but out of it all true religion is destined to emerge in undiminished luster, as gold from the purifying furnace. In the meanwhile let us say with Samuel, "Jehovah is God and Jehovah is my Father." Let us hold fast, above all, to the unchanging love of our Father, who loves us with a love with which there is nothing to compare in heaven or earth.

Samuel knew that there were two objectives which must be realized before Israel's sad condition could be remedied or the divine ideal realized. *First: The national unity must be recovered from the anarchy in which it had been overwhelmed.* It was useless to think of holding the land against the inroads of the neighboring people so long as each tribe was content with an isolated existence, repelling its own enemies for a time but indifferent to the condition of its neighbors and of the country at large. Israel must be one, animated by a common enthusiasm for its future independence and integrity. Let each tribe be proud of its idiosyncrasy and fulfill its own distinctive mission; but let all be one in asserting the independence and glory of the chosen people.

This is no less desirable in our own age. The divisions of the Church are her bane and render her impotent before her foes. Ephraim envies Judah, and Judah vexes Ephraim; and their common enemies make profit out of their mutual recriminations and rivalries. It is a sad spectacle to witness the divisions between Christians in the face of a mocking world, and we shall never be able to make men believe until we have learned to magnify the points of agreement and to bear with all those who love the Lord Jesus and are united with Him as their living Head, though their method of stating the truth may differ widely from our own.

Second: The evils that had eaten into the nation's heart must be put away. The people had forsaken the God of their fathers for the Phoenician and Philistine deities, whose images were worshiped in His stead. Shrines to Baal and Ashtaroth covered the land. Foul orgies of shameless impurity were everywhere rife. And it was evident that only a widespread revival of religion could save the people from rotting away before the very evils for which the ancient Canaanites had been destroyed.

Samuel was preeminently a man of prayer. He is known on the subsequent pages of Scripture as he that called on the Divine Name (1 Sam. 9:6–9; Ps. 99:6; Jer. 15:1). In addition, he was a man of blameless reputation and life—in themselves eminent qualifications. It has been truly said that the special work of guiding, moderating and softening the jarring counsels of men is the particular privilege of those who have grown up into natural strength from the early beginnings of purity and goodness; of those who can humbly and thankfully look back through middle age, and youth, and childhood, with no sudden rent or breach to their pure and peaceful recollections—and such was certainly Samuel's happy lot. He was also a man of practical sagacity, and by his appeals wrought upon the national conscience; so that, as the result of his efforts, "it came to pass, while the ark abode in Kirjath-jearim, that the time was long; for it was twenty years: and all the house of Israel lamented before the Lord."

Notice those two phrases: *all* the house of Israel—there is the restoration of the lost unity; *lamented* before the Lord—there is the national repentance, which was followed by a widespread reformation: "Then the children of Israel did put away Baalim and Ashtaroth, and served the Lord only." Would that there might be a similar turning unto God in our own time and land! "Revive, O Lord, Thy work in the midst of the years. In the midst of the years make known."

7

THE VICTORY OF FAITH

(1 Samuel 7:1–14)

"Oh bring us back once more
The vanished days of yore,
When the world with faith was filled!
Bring back the fervid zeal,
The hearts of fire and steel,
The hands that believe and build."

LONGFELLOW

AFTER twenty years of quiet and unobtrusive toil, Samuel had led his people to desire both to feel and manifest the old unity which had made them one before their enemies, and there was a distinct yearning after Jehovah. The sacred writer tells us that all the house of Israel "was drawn together" after Jehovah (7:2, R.V. margin). In being drawn to God they were drawn towards each other, as the spokes of a wheel center in the hub. If the Lord Jesus is the center of our heart-life, we must inevitably be drawn into fellowship with all those to whom He is also first and best.

In verses 3 and 4 we probably have the substance of innumerable exhortations which Samuel delivered to all the house of Israel. From end to end he traversed the country, urging the people to return to Jehovah; to put away the false gods and Ashtaroth, and to direct their hearts to the God of their fathers and serve Him only. Wherever he could find a group of willing listeners, he poured forth his prayers and tears, his rugged denunciations of sin, and his fervent exhortations to a true repentance. Now he would stand upon the historic site of Jericho; then he might be found on the ancient heights of Carmel, Shiloh, Nob or Hebron, witnessing to vast gatherings of deeply moved and repentant people; and finally, as the result of all that he had said, there was a great turning to God. On every hand idols were cast from their pedestals, and the vicious orgies were brought to an end in the groves and valleys. It was as though the spirit of spring were breathing over some wintry waste, and through the thawing snow the grass and flowers began to appear. Oh, that Samuels by the score might be raised up to induce the Church of God to put away what grieves Him, with the assurance that when she has arrayed herself in the beautiful garments of humility and purity, God will deliver her out of the hands of the Philistines.

I. THE CONVOCATION AT MIZPEH.—The movement to which we have referred at last demanded a public demonstration, and Samuel summoned all Israel to Mizpeh—which means *watchtower,* and is evidently a commanding summit that can still be identified in central Palestine, rising some five hundred feet above the surrounding country and nearly three thousand above the sea level. It is remarkable that on the summit of this hill, as at Shiloh and Kirjath-jearim, there is a level platform some five or six feet high, cut out of the rock, where doubtless some kind of building was erected to receive the sacred tent.

The day was devoted to fasting, as the law enjoined on the great Day of Atonement. The people confessed their sins, afflicted their souls, and humbled themselves before Jehovah. In addition, a somewhat novel rite was introduced. Water was brought from a neighboring well, and solemnly poured out before the Lord (v. 6), as afterwards at the Feast of Tabernacles. Whenever that great festival had nearly run its course, as it was being celebrated in the temple, it was the custom for the priests to go forth to the Spring of Siloam, accompanied by the Levite choir, and bring thence water in a golden vessel; this was poured out at the foot of the altar at the hour of the morning sacrifice, while all around the white-vestured choir chanted Isaiah's words, "With joy shall ye draw water out of the wells of salvation." Whether this scene in the life of Samuel was the origin of that solemn procession, it is impossible to say. Such may have been the case, though it is generally assumed that, as used in the temple service, the pouring out of water was a memorial of the flowing of water from the smitten rock in the wilderness, and the type of the pouring out of the Holy Spirit (John 7:37–39).

The pouring forth of water may have implied that they poured forth from their full hearts floods of penitence and tears; that they desired by the heaviness of their grief to wash their land free from the accumulated evil of the past years; or that the people realized their utter helplessness, so that they were as water spilt on the ground, which could not be gathered up. But whatever it may have signified, it must have been a very striking spectacle, when Samuel, as the representative of his countrymen, brought the whole nation back to true loyal allegiance to the God of their fathers. It was a worthy act for his manhood's prime, and we are not surprised to learn that, as by a sudden outburst of acclamation, he was appointed judge (v. 6).

Oh, who shall induce the professing Church of God to put away the evil things by which her testimony is now impaired! Sometimes in buildings connected with the Church we hear of fancy-fairs, raffles, full-dress soirees, dances, theatricals, comic concerts, and many other such little things, which indicate the corruption of the spiritual life as certainly as an army of fungi indicate the damp and unwholesome atmosphere in which they thrive. What would not be the blessed result if the children of God would come to another Mizpeh and confess, as Israel did, "We have sinned against the Lord!"

II. THE VICTORY OF FAITH.—The tidings of this great convocation reached the Philistines, who looked upon it as an unmistakable sign of the returning spirit of national life, and "the lords of the Philistines went up against Israel" (v. 7). From every part the contingents of a great army were assembled, and there was every reason to fear that the terrible experiences of Aphek would be renewed. A panic of fear spread through the multitudes of Israel. There appeared but one hope: God must arise to His people's help, or they would be trampled as the leaves of autumn beneath the heel of the conqueror. What could timid sheep do against wolves? What could unarmed peasants do against such soldiers? How could the national life, which was just reviving after the discouragement and anarchy of years, withstand the onset of these bitter foes? "Cease not to cry unto the Lord our God for us," the people said to Samuel, "that He will save us out of the hand of the Philistines."

Ah, soul! this is the only hope for thee. Thou hast been ground down beneath tyrant sins, which have held thee in subjection as the Philistines did Israel; thou hast groaned in the prison house like another Samson shorn of his locks. There seems no help or hope of deliverance, because thy moral life is impaired by the commission of evils analogous to those which infected the Hebrew nation in the days of the judges. Only put these away and stand clear of them; in the name of God pour out all your self-confidence before the cross where Jesus died, receive the forgiveness which is never withheld from the penitent and believing soul; and then, however many be the obstacles, temptations and sins that beset thee, know that the Lord will save thee out of the hand of thine enemies.

If only the tempted and overwhelmed would bathe their souls in the purifying waters of the Word of God and cultivate the spirit of unwavering prayer and faith, the Lord would fight for them and they could then hold their peace.

When so far as we know them we have put away our sins, or at least are steadfastly resolved to be rid of them, we may count on an ungrieved Holy Spirit; and this always means the consciousness of our Saviour's presence as our deliverer from the power of the enemy.

The power of Samuel's prayers was already known throughout the land, like those of John Knox in the days of Queen Mary. The people had come to believe in them; they felt them to be the palladium of their liberties. If only Samuel would pray, they might count on deliverance. They knew that he had prayed; they now entreated that he would not cease.

But Samuel did more than pray. He took a sucking lamb and offered it as a whole burnt offering to the Lord, symbolizing thus the desire of Israel to be wholly yielded to the divine will. There must be consecration before there can be faith and deliverance. It is not enough simply to put away sin; we must also give ourselves absolutely and entirely to God. There must be a wholeness in the offering, the yielding of ourselves—spirit, soul and body—to be whatever God would have us be. Failure in the walk always denotes failure in the heart-life. If you are perpetually overcome by the Philistines, be sure that there is a flaw in your inner consecration.

While the smoke of this offering was rising in the calm air and the eyes of tens of thousands were fixed upon the figure of Samuel, who, as a prophet of the Lord, was within his rights in superseding the Levitical priests in this solemn function, and while his piercing cries for divine help were rising to heaven, the Philistines drew near to battle against Israel. Can you not see them creeping up the mountain slopes and encircling the defenseless crowd which had no might nor power to resist? But suddenly the voice of God answered the voice of the prophet. "The Lord thundered with a great thunder [Hebrew, *voice*] on that day upon the Philistines, and discomfited them." The sky was suddenly black with tempest, peal after peal rolled through the mountains, the heart of the foe was stricken with terror, and though Israel drew never a sword, the heathen turned in dismay to flee. Then at a signal from Samuel, the men of Israel flung themselves upon the flying foe. Down the steep they sped, catching up the arms which were cast away in flight, and stripping the dead of their weapons. Josephus tells of another circumstance that added to the horrors of that irresistible onslaught. "God destroyed their ranks with an earthquake; the ground trembled under their feet, so that there was no place whereon to stand in safety. They either fell helpless to the earth, or into some of the chasms that opened beneath them."

The pursuit ended only when the Philistines came beneath the shadow of their own fortress of Beth-car, House of Pasture— known today as the Well of the Vineyards.

This is the great message of the whole story for us. If only the Church of God would put away the evils that grieve His Holy Spirit, if only we would ourselves come out and be separate, not touching the unclean thing, and cleansing ourselves from all filthiness of the flesh, the Spirit would interpose for us too. The Lord would deliver us, fighting on our behalf against our foes, so that we would be more than conquerors through Him that loveth us and have to do nothing more than take the spoil.

III. The Stone of Help.—"Then Samuel took a stone, and set it between Mizpeh and Shen, and called it Ebenezer [the stone of help] saying, 'Hitherto hath the Lord helped us.'" This was the same spot upon which Israel had suffered the great defeat which led to the capture of the ark (4:1). How wonderful this was, that the story of the victory should be told upon the plain which had been the scene of defeat! Does not this carry sweet encouragement? Is it not true that when we turn to God, the disgrace of our failure is blotted out in the glory of our deliverance, so that we talk no more of our sins and their fatal consequences but only of God and His almighty succor? Yes, child of God, be aware that the place of defeat may become that of victory, sublime and glorious so as to fill your heart with adoring rapture, and heaven with consenting praise. Think how, in the generations that succeeded, fathers brought their children to look at that great stone and read the inscription, "Hitherto hath the Lord helped us," arguing from it that what He had done He would do—that the forgiveness and grace which He had shown upon that site would be renewed and repeated in all after-years.

From that moment Samuel's supremacy in the country was established. The Philistines came no more during his judgeship within the border of Israel. The hand of the Lord was against the Philistines all his days. The alienated cities which the Philistines had taken from Israel were restored to Israel, from Ekron even unto Gath. Even the Amorites, who had taken part with the Canaanites, found it to their advantage to side with Samuel and abstain from hostilities (v. 14). As Dean Spence, in Ellicott's *Commentary*, says, "This success at Ebenezer was no mere solitary victory, but was the sign of a new spirit in Israel, which animated the nation during the lifetime of Samuel, and the reigns of David and Solomon and of the great Hebrew kings. The petty jealousies had disappeared, and had given place to a great national desire for unity. The old idol worship of Canaan, which degraded every nationality which practiced it, was in a great measure swept away from among the chosen people, while the pure religion of the Lord of hosts was established, not only through the care and guardianship of the tribe of Levi, but by the new order of the prophets."

What cannot prayer do? It can not only open and close heaven, but will give the soul that prays an undisputed supremacy over his times, so that men will acknowledge that the savior of the city is not so much the politician, the man of intellect, or the man of affairs, but he who has learned how to walk with God, and by his character and intercession to be the safeguard of the national liberties and existence.

8

THE STONE OF HELP

(1 Samuel 7:12)

"And in the strength of this I rode,
Shattering all evil customs everywhere,
And past thro' Pagan realms, and made them mine,
And clash'd with Pagan hordes, and bore them down,
And broke thro' all, and in the strength of this
Came Victor."

TENNYSON

THERE are many such monoliths as the "Stone of Help" to be found strewn through these northern lands, from such venerable circles as those of Stonehenge to the single ones which are pointed out to the traveler in northern Wales—the last home of the Druids and ancient Britons.

Throughout the world man has endeavored to associate himself, and the history of his life, with the permanent monuments of nature. In this he has shown alike his littleness and his greatness—*his littleness*, because every such endeavor is a confession on his part of the transience of his days and his consciousness that he has so slight a hold on the earth, on which he is but a sojourner and a pilgrim; his greatness, because he is capable of investing with a halo of undying interest wild glens and barren rocks, darksome caves and deep, rushing rivers. It is for this reason that every spot in the older countries of the world teems with interest. It is with difficulty that the tourist can make his way headlong through England or Scotland, Germany or Italy; whereas he will haste, without hesitation or halting, through thousands of miles of Canada or Siberia. How different, for instance, is the interest of traveling through the New England States from going through North Dakota. Each square mile of the former is fragrant with some interesting reminiscence of the past, while the other only recalls a vanquished race.

At the foot of this stone let us linger for a little, to learn one or two lessons more. For stones have ears and voices. Joshua said that the stone which he reared, at the end of his lifework, had *heard*; and our Lord said that the stones around Him might be expected to cry out (Josh. 24:27; Luke 19:40).

I. ITS SITE.—It stood on ground which had witnessed a terrible defeat and disaster. We are told in the fourth chapter that the great battle of Aphek was fought on this spot. "Israel went out against the Philistines to battle, and pitched beside Ebenezer, and the Philistines pitched in Aphek." "Now the Philistines had taken the ark of God, and they brought it from Ebenezer unto Ashdod" (4:1; 5:1).

Many who gathered around Samuel when he raised and named this stone must have been present twenty years before on that fatal field, the Flodden of Israel's glory. Here the fight had been fiercest, the slain thickest; there the corpses of Hebrews and Philistines had fallen like leaves in Vallombrosa, trampled beneath the feet of the combatants; yonder the fight had raged around the ark of God, as it was taken, and retaken, and taken again. At this point, desperate deeds of valor had been done to turn back Israel from a shameful flight, but in vain. There Hophni fell, and there Phinehas. In this place a brief stand was made, but again the ill-formed line was broken, and the children of a chosen race, whose forefathers turned not back in the days of Gideon and Jephthah, fled like sheep before the wolf.

But, not withstanding all this, and though the spot was associated with the memories of disgrace and shame, which in turn were the result of deep transgression on the part of people and priesthood, yet there was the stone erected which spoke so eloquently of the divine help.

What living encouragement is contained in this for us all! We, too, may be traversing at this very hour battlefields which have been sadly marked by defeat. Again and again we have met the foes of our peace in mortal conflict, only to be repulsed. Our hopes have been dashed to the ground and our banners rolled in dust and blood. We meant never to yield again, but we did yield. We meant that that solemn vow should be kept, that holy resolution carried into effect; but they were shivered in pieces. We have been overthrown by our adversary and overpowered in spite of all our efforts by our besetting sin. Yet take heart. At the very place where you have fallen you shall stand, for "God is able to make you stand"; where you have been overthrown you shall be more than a conqueror. You shall tread these very fields with songs of joy. The rocks which saw the withered leaves of autumn swirl in eddies around you shall behold the young green of spring and the mature fullness of summer. Be of good cheer! The stone of Ebenezer shall be raised on the very field of the fatal battle of Aphek.

II. Its Retrospect.—What a story this stone had to tell, if all were unfolded, of the wonderful dealings of God with His people. It looked back on the twenty years of patient work by which the prophet Samuel had been leading the people homeward to the God of their fathers—quiet, unobtrusive and unseen work, like that of the coral insects from the bottom of the mighty ocean, till presently the islet emerges, with its crown of fronded palms.

It looked back on many a scene of iconoclasm as, from Dan to Beer-sheba, there had been a general putting away of the Baalim and Ashtaroth, the cutting down of groves and overthrow of altars. It looked back on that memorable convocation of all Israel at Mizpeh, when water was poured out before the Lord in confession of sin and humble penitence.

It looked back, specially, to the offering of the burnt offering, which declared Israel's resolve to be henceforth wholly devoted to God, and to Samuel's piercing cry of intercession. Above all, it looked back on that memorable moment, when, as the Philistines drew near to battle against Israel, "the Lord thundered with a great thunder upon the Philistines, and discomfited them, and they were smitten down before Israel." If that stone had engraved slabs of memory within its old heart, as well as eyes and ears, it surely never would forget the mad onslaught of the men of Israel on their fleeing and panic-stricken foes, to avenge in one brief hour the wrongs and oppressions of twenty long years.

Has anything like this taken place in your life? On your answer much will depend. If since your last failure and defeat there have been no acts of the soul like those which took place at Mizpeh, believe me, there is no probability of there being any break in the long monotony of your reverses. As you have been defeated, so you will be defeated; as you have failed, so you will fail, unless there is the pouring out of your heart before God, the putting away of idols, and the resolve to follow Him fully.

If I may be permitted to quote my own experience, I must bear witness to the incessant failure of my life so long as I cherished things in my heart which were alien to God's holy will. Rules for holy living, solemn and heart-stirring conventions, helpful books and addresses produced but very small result. There was temporary amendment, but little else. But when the scene at Mizpeh had been reflected in the inner mirror of the soul, then victory took place on the very spot marked by defeat. Let my reader ponder this. You cannot keep the moth out of your house as long as one old blanket, stored in some neglected cupboard or box, is full of larva. You cannot keep diphtheria from your home as long as one crack in the drains is emitting the poison of sewer gas. You will never raise your stone of Ebenezer until you have stood on the watchtower of Mizpeh and put away all known sin, all complicity with what is grievous in the eyes of Christ. Only so will even His keeping power avail.

You say that you cannot. The evil thing clings to you as the serpent folds around Laocoon and his sons. The deadly creeper has wound itself around the tree of your life and threatens to crush it to death in its deadly embrace. How can you rid yourself of that which has so strong a fascination that you feel you cannot live apart from it? Ah, that is the point where the Great Physician is willing to interpose for your rescue and deliverance! What you cannot do for yourself, He will do. The only question is, *Are you willing?* or *Are you willing to be made willing?* Often enough in the history of the soul it happens that the will, like a tough piece of iron, resists and resents. Then there is one glad resource—take it to Christ, tell Him that you cannot be as you would, or that you will not be as you should, and pray Him to undertake your difficult and almost desperate case.

Do not doubt the result. He takes what we give at the moment of our giving it; and when once He has taken it, we may press to our heart the consolation which the good Naomi gave to Ruth in a memorable moment of her life: "Sit still, my daughter, . . . for the man will not rest until he has finished the thing this day."

III. Its Inscription.—"Hitherto hath the Lord helped us." Surely if the stone had a retrospect, as we have seen, it had also a prospect. It looked forward as well as backward. It seemed to say, "As God has helped, so He will help." It would have been impossible to secure such results as those twenty years had witnessed, culminating in this glorious victory, unless He had been a very present help; and could He have done so much without being prepared to finish what He had commenced? Would He have begun to build without calculating on His ability to finish? Would He have entered on a campaign without counting the cost of carrying it to a conclusion?

As we go through life, let us be careful to erect our Ebenezer stones, so that when new responsibilities begin to crowd on us, or fresh and unforeseen difficulties threaten, we may be emboldened to sing with Newton:

> *"His love in time past forbids me to think*
> *He'll leave me at last in trouble to sink,*
> *Each sweet Ebenezer I have in review*
> *Confirms His good pleasure to help me quite through."*

All through life, if you will only trust God, if only by faith you will derive from Him grace for grace, if only you will claim a continuance and a crowning of all that He has begun, you will have occasions to raise these stones of help and to say with the apostle, "Having, therefore, obtained the help that is from God, I stand unto this day testifying both to small and great." The last stone that we shall erect will be on the margin of the river. As we turn our back forever on the land of our pilgrimage and enter on the work and worship of eternity, we shall set up a great stone to the glory of our God, saying once more, with a deep sigh of perfected satisfaction, "Hitherto hath the Lord helped."

9

A GREAT DISAPPOINTMENT

(1 Samuel 7–8)

"They who have steeped their souls in prayer
Can every anguish calmly bear—
They who have learned to pray aright
From pain's dark well draw up delight."

HOUGHTON

THE supreme test of character is disappointment and apparent failure. When the flowing stream is with us, and our plans are ripening into fruition, it is easy enough to be at our best. But what we really are does not appear under such conditions. Let the tide turn against us, let men avert their faces and refuse our counsels, let us be driven to stand on the defense against a world in arms—then our true mettle is approved. We are now to see how Samuel bore himself in the face of a keen disappointment. This at least may be said of him, as of old it was said of Job, that he still held fast his integrity.

I. HOW THE DISAPPOINTMENT BEFELL.—During the twenty years that followed the glorious victory of Aphek, Samuel set himself to build up in the hearts of his fellow countrymen something of that profound belief in the reign of the Divine King which we know as the theocracy, and which was so dear to all devout Hebrews.

His headquarters and home were at Ramah, the scene of his happy childhood years. From there he went on itinerating journeys, and *wherever he traveled, Samuel strove to act only as the representative and agent of the Divine King.* Who was he but the messenger and minister of the Lord of hosts? With all the force of his character and eloquence of his speech he insisted that the people were the subjects of Jehovah, owing allegiance to Him alone, and receiving from Him direction in times of perplexity and deliverance in days of battle. They needed no king—Jehovah was King; no officials but those who uttered His messages; no code of laws but those that emanated from Him. It was a beautiful and inspiring conception; and as he went to and fro throughout the land of Israel, still upon his lips, like a musical refrain, the words were constantly being breathed, "Speak, Lord, for Thy servant heareth."

The same object was in his mind as he instituted the schools of the prophets. To Samuel's wise interpretation of his times we must attribute the institution of these seats of learning. The priesthood had forfeited its right to stand between Jehovah and His people. Eli and his sons had failed too abjectly and entirely to realize the purpose for which their office was instituted in order to expect any resuscitation of the priestly order. It was clear that some other religious body must be called into existence. The times demanded an order of men who would be trained in the law of God, who would be fitted to interpret the holy oracles to the people, and from the midst of whom men should arise from time to time to tell in the light what they had heard in the darkness, to proclaim on the housetops what God had whispered to their ears in secret. We find these schools flourishing in the days of Elijah and Elisha—some apparently on the same sites where they had been instituted by Samuel (10:3–5; 19:23–24; 2 Kings 2).

As Samuel laboriously built up these institutions he had but one purpose in his heart. It was his eager desire to imbue the minds of his countrymen with his own sublime conceptions of the

Divine Kingship; and how would he do it better than by these young and ardent disciples? And it must have been a constant inspiration to them to live in contact with this great and illustrious man, who was statesman and saint in one, whom they revered for the loftiness of his character while they felt the inspiration of his high ideals. They saw how respected he was in his own city by young and old (9:12–13); how accessible he was to all who needed his assistance (v. 9); how mightily he wrestled and prevailed in prayer (7:17; 8:10, 21) and they counted it their highest honor to be associated with him in the regeneration of their national life.

But the failure to realize his high purpose seems to have befallen through the failure of his sons. As Samuel became old, he was less able to administer justice and continue to act as the adviser of his people in their natural and domestic affairs. The burden of administering the government, in the name of the unseen King, became too heavy for him, and he appointed his sons to assist him on the extreme frontiers of the South country. The experiment of delegating to them a part of his authority proved, however, to be a disastrous failure. "They walked not in his ways, but turned aside after lucre, and took bribes, and perverted justice."

This precipitated the catastrophe; and "all the elders of Israel," who evidently formed a kind of representative and popular assembly, came to Samuel at Ramah, to urge that he should make more satisfactory and permanent arrangements for the perpetuation of his authority. They said to him, "Behold, thou art old, and thy sons walk not in thy ways; now make us a king to judge us like all the nations."

Looked at from the human standpoint, there was much to warrant the request. The Philistines were pushing their outposts into the heart of the country (13:3–5); Nahash, the Ammonite, was a dangerous neighbor on the eastern frontier (11:1); there was fear that disintegration might again separate the people on Samuel's death. But, on the other hand, the request shattered the prophet's hopes. It showed him that his ideal was too lofty and spiritual for the people to appreciate and maintain. They could not believe only in the invisible, they must have the outward symbols and splendor of royalty.

This is the universal failure of the heart of man. It is always craving for the sensuous and visible. Like the children of Israel, with their cry, "Make us gods, which may go before us," men demand something which they may see and handle and before which they may prostrate themselves. Hence all spiritual worship shows a tendency to become materialistic. It is hard to believe that God is a Spirit, and that He must be worshiped in spirit and in truth; it is easier to enter into the debate whether "in this mountain or in Jerusalem men ought to worship."

These paragraphs are being written in a land where this fact is strikingly illustrated. The national church was the earliest product of apostolic days—the church of Athanasius, Cyril and Chrysostom. From the first it recited the prayers and read the Scriptures in the tongue of the people, eschewed images, and insisted on spiritual worship. Yet now its churches are full of the pictures of the saints, before which women burn candles and men cross themselves; the Holy of Holies is shut off from the common foot by golden gates; the deep bass of the reader mingles with the exquisite voices of boys in rendering the service in an almost unknown tongue—everything that can appeal to the sense is called into requisition. Apparently the people love to have it so, for they stand in dense crowds on the spacious pavements, following each invocation of the Divine Name with profuse genuflections and obeisance. As I turn from these ornate and splendid symbols to other gatherings of God's people in which the eye has nothing to allure or the ear to attract, where the thought is centered on God and the only splendor is in those great conceptions that elevate and ennoble, I do not wonder that the nature of the ordinary man rebels and cries out for something more suited to the common levels of daily experience.

To combat desires like these the Epistle to the Hebrews was written, that our minds and hearts might thither ascend and continually dwell where the Lord has gone before us. For us, not a mount that can be touched but a mount not less certainly—Mount Zion; not a city whose minarets and monuments catch the rays of the rising and setting sun, but a city as surely, whose streets we may walk each day—the heavenly Jerusalem; not the festal crowds of worshipers that jostled each other in their climb to the temple of Solomon, but fellow worshipers equally real and numerous—the innumerable hosts of angels, the spirits of just men made perfect, the general assembly and church of the firstborn, with whom we come into contact at each hour of prayer.

II. HOW SAMUEL BORE HIS DISAPPOINTMENT.—"The thing displeased Samuel when they said, 'Give us a king to judge us.'" It was not so much that they had rejected himself, but that they had rejected God—that He should not be King over them. They had failed to grasp the great conception and had fallen to the level of the nations around. The one hope that had arisen in his soul, and been nurtured by the dew and sun of every summer, was frustrated; and it was clear that there could never be the realization of his cherished dream, since it was impossible to imagine circumstances more favorable for giving it effect. If it failed in Israel, it would fail entirely—unless, indeed, the Divine Kingdom could be set up, which would never pass away.

Under these bitter circumstances he made for the one harbor of refuge, the one assured safeguard for all broken hearts and wrecked lives, for all that labor and are heavy laden—"Samuel prayed unto the Lord."

By how many disappointed ones these words may be read! Women whose young hearts were filled on their marriage day with high and buoyant hope, as they dreamed of an ideal life of love and blessedness, but who are mourning over the withered vows, the broken promises, the irrecoverable sense of trust and peace! Men that meant to effect such great things by their lives, to succeed in business, to lead society, to mold and fashion the State! Ministers who, as they knelt on the threshold of their sacred calling, saw visions and dreamed dreams of consecration, tenderness, shepherd-care and parental solicitude which have vanished as the pictures of foliage reflected in deep lakes when a breath of wind stirs the surface of the water! What are such to do? Whither can they go? What resort is there for broken hearts?

There is no answer to these questions but that suggested by Samuel's action, when he prayed unto the Lord. Go to Him, and tell everything—what you hoped, how you endeavored, how you failed. Weep your tears out at His feet. He can understand, can sympathize, can bind and heal. There is Balm in Gilead, there is a Physician there. There is help for the helpless and comfort for the comfortless. To tell God everything is to be far along the road to peace; and where you cannot tell, where the sobs choke the utterance, there the Father seeth, knoweth and comforteth. Through His love you may be as one whom his mother comforteth.

Then the Lord answered His servant. He always does, and will, answer. The voice may be so soft and low as to be almost inaudible, but it will be there. The words may not quite chime in with our notions at first. Unlike the prophet Exekiel's scroll, they may be bitter in the mouth, but they will be sweet to the heart. "Be careful for nothing, but in everything by prayer and supplication, with thanksgiving let your requests be made known unto God, and the peace of God that passeth all understanding shall guard your hearts and your thoughts in Christ Jesus."

III. THE DIVINE ANSWER AND ENCOURAGEMENT.—When Samuel cried to the Lord about his sore trouble, in the divine answer it was made clear that the cherished ideal of a lifetime would have to be abandoned. The distinct impression was borne in on the prophet's mind that he must renounce his high purpose, abdicate his position, and step down to become subordinate to a king. "Now, therefore," said his Almighty Friend and Confidant, "hearken unto their voice."

At the same time his sorrow was greatly mitigated by discovering that God was his fellow Sufferer, and that the sorrow of the divine heart was infinitely greater than his own. "They have not rejected thee, *but they have rejected Me.*" It is a great honor when a man is summoned to enter into fellowship with God in the awful pain and grief which men bring on His tender and holy Spirit.

Surely none will count the phrase extravagant which attributes suffering to God on account of His rejection by human hearts which refuse His reign and do despite to the Spirit of His grace. Did not Jesus suffer when His own received Him not, when His brethren believed not, when the city, which He loved with patriot devotion, refused to shelter under His shadowing wings, and when His chosen apostles forsook Him and fled? The very abandonment of His self-sacrifice proved the tenderness of His yearning love, and this could not have been present to so large an extent within Him without exposing Him to excessive suffering on account of human sin. It has been beautifully said by a modern writer: "There is a common saying that cruelty and cowardice go together; so also do self-sacrifice and tenderness. They are different sides of the same idea, and all the delicacy of Christian tenderness is perceptibly an outgrowth of the Cross. It seems as though, till Christ had lived and died, that fullness of human sympathy was impossible." Now, if that be true—if the Cross of Christ has exhaled through the world the aroma of tender sympathy—how strong this element must have been in His holy nature, and how acutely He must have suffered when the keepers of the vineyards cast Him out and slew Him. But He did not suffer alone; they that saw Him saw the Father. He taught us that God was not impassive; but that He yearned, sorrowed, loved, as human fathers do, only with heights and depths of intensity which are indeed divine.

> "*Thou who hast borne all burdens, bear our load,*
> *Bear Thou our load, whatever load it be;*
> *Our guilt, our shame, our helpless misery,*
> *Bear Thou who only canst, O God, my God,*
> *Seek us and find us, for we cannot Thee.*"

The prophet says that God was pressed beneath the sin and rebellion of men, as the groaning wagon is pressed beneath its sheaves.

IV. SAMUEL'S NOBLE BEHAVIOR TOWARDS THE PEOPLE DEMANDS OUR NOTICE.

The request of the people for a king was, no doubt, in part based on Deuteronomy 17:14, which seemed to anticipate just such a crisis as had now arisen. In Hannah's song, also, there had been an unmistakable prophecy of the day when Jehovah would give strength to His king and exalt the horn of His anointed (1 Sam. 2:10). But the present request had been sprung on Samuel prematurely, and with undue passion and haste. Instead of seeking to ascertain the mind of God, the people had made up their own mind; instead of consulting with the aged prophet on the best policy for coming days, they dictated the policy on which they had set their hearts.

Under these circumstances, and with the express direction of God, he protested solemnly to the deputation of elders, and through them to the people, showing the manner of the king that would reign. It was impossible that a king demanded in such a spirit as characterized the people could be a man after God's own heart. They wanted one who, in his stature and bearing, in his martial prowess and deeds, should be worthy to compare with neighboring monarchs. This was much more to them than character, obedience to God, or loyalty to the Mosaic code. And as they desired, so it was done unto them. Ah, how often it happens that God grants us according to the insistence of our strong and vehement self-will. He gives us according to our request, but sends leanness into our souls (Ps. 106:15).

All the Oriental extravagance and prodigality of human life, which were the familiar accompaniment of royalty in neighboring countries, were destined to reappear in the court of the kings of Israel. They would enforce the service of the young men to fabricate their weapons, fight their battles, and minister to their royal state. They would exact unremunerated labor in the tillage of their lands. From the daughters and wives of the people they would demand confectioneries and pastries, and other elaborate luxuries for the royal appetite. Vineyards and olive yards, farms and lands, would be confiscated at their caprice. A system of heavy taxation would be imposed on the produce of the land, and on the flocks and herds which covered the pasture lands; while the people would have to stand still and see their hard-earned money squandered on the pleasures and self-indulgence of the palace. A brief experience of this kind would lead to a universal outcry as the nation awoke to its grievous mistake; but the step so rashly taken would be found to be irreparable. "Ye shall cry out in that day because of your king which ye shall have chosen you; and the Lord will not answer you in that day."

Samuel's protest and remonstrance were, however, alike in vain. "The people refused to hearken unto the voice of Samuel; and they said, 'Nay, but we will have a king over us, that we also may be like all the nations, and that our king may judge us, and go out before us and fight our battles.'" They trusted in man and in the arm of flesh, their heart departed from the Lord, and in the sequel they were destined to see their king slain on the fatal field of Gilboa, their land overrun by the enemy, and the national fortunes reduced to the lowest possible ebb.

Does your heart cry out for a king, for one who shall reduce the conflicting passions of your nature to unity and order? Beware lest you choose after the sight of your eyes or the hearing of your ears; let not sense or appetite make the selection; take heed of the lust of your flesh, the lust of your eyes, and the pride of your life!

I was told, when in Russia, that in one of the villages in the Baltic provinces a man is imprisoned in the strong bars of an iron cage, who approaches each person on entering the chamber where it is fixed, and, presenting a silver ruble, says, "This is God." Very few state the truth so boldly; but of how many such a statement would express the very fact? Let your king be the man whom God has chosen, the Man of Calvary, whom He has exalted to be a Prince and a Saviour. He will not exact *from* but bring *to* you. He does not impoverish, but enrich. His scepter is the broken reed; His steed, a foal; His crown, of thorns!

When Samuel saw that the people had made up their mind he dismissed the assembly and set himself with remarkable magnanimity to do the best he could for them. He did this in obedience to the divine summons, which lay along the line of his own thoughts.

This is very remarkable and justifies the remark of Ewald: "Samuel is one of the few great men in history who, in critical times, by sheer force of character and inimitable energy, terminate the previous form of a great existing system—at first against their own will, but afterwards, when convinced of the necessity, with all the force and eagerness of their nature; and who then initiate a better form with the happiest results, amid much personal suffering and persecution."

During the early years of his life, and well on into the maturity of his power, Samuel sought to vitalize the existing institutions, which were ready to his hands. Only slowly, and against his wishes, he awoke to realize that he must abandon further efforts in this direction, and set himself to build up an entirely new organization. In doing this he had to sacrifice his previous convictions and do violence to his better judgment; he had to pull down the very structure that he had been at such pains to establish; he had to be second, where he had been an unchallenged first. But when once he realized that there was no alternative, he became the most devoted and efficient organizer of the new age; just as Dr. Chalmers, when he found that it was impossible to secure what he sought within the borders of the established Church of Scotland, stepped out from its pale and began to build the Free Church, which has become one of the greatest churches of the age.

" And," continues Ewald, "if David's visible deeds are greater or more dazzling than Samuel's, still there can be no doubt that David's blaze of glory would have been impossible without Samuel's less conspicuous but far more influential career; so that all the greatness of which the following century boasts goes back to him as its real author."

There are supreme crises in the lives of some of us which search us to the quick. The people whom we have loved, have suffered and sacrificed for, suddenly turn from us. They want something else and something more. We realize that we must abdicate and are tempted to do it with grudging courtesy and an ill grace. Why should we make way for others; why renounce our rights and refuse to press our claims?

At such times let us remember Samuel's heroism; let us acknowledge that God's will is leading us by a right way; let us care for the flock over which we have been placed as overseers more than we care for ourselves; let us adapt ourselves to the new order; nay, let us expedite it with all the grace and grit that we can command, knowing that the blood of our self-sacrifice will, by God's blessing, be the best cement of our handiwork.

10

THE VOICE OF CIRCUMSTANCES

(1 Samuel 9–10)

> " *Yes! thou dost well to build a fence about*
> *Thine inward faith. Oh, mount a stalwart guard*
> *Of answers, to oppose invading doubt.*
> *All aids are needful, for the strife is hard.*"
>
> COLERIDGE

"WHOSO is wise and will observe these things, even he shall understand the lovingkindness of the Lord." In these words the Psalmist sums up his five tableaux of human life (Ps. 107). The track of the pilgrim host, the experience of the prisoner languishing in his chains, the recovery of the sick from long depression, the deliverance of the storm-tossed crew from the angry breakers, the evolution of a smiling paradise from an arid and parched wilderness—all these things, if carefully observed, yield their testimony and assurance that God is in all events, permitting, directing, controlling and causing all things to work out His perfect plan.

In all Scripture there is no passage more illustrative of this than the chapters before us, which show how clearly and mightily God is in the circumstances of our lives.

It was the spring of the day. With exquisite clearness and purity the dawn was breaking in the eastern sky, when three men descended the steep ascent on which Ramah stood, and emerged from the city gate (vv. 11–12, 14, 27). The group was a remarkable one, comprising the aged seer, "a young man and a goodly"—who was the king-elect, though he did not realize it—and a herdsman, Doeg (so tradition states), who afterwards attained such an unhappy notoriety but was at that time simply a servant in attendance on his master's son. When the city gate had been left behind, the servant was sent on in front that he might not be a witness to the solemn transaction, which inaugurated a new epoch in the life of Saul. "As they were going down at the end of the city, Samuel said to Saul, 'Bid thy servant pass on before us, but stand thou still at this time, that I may cause thee to hear the word of God.'"

I. The Circumstances That Led Up to This Incident.— (1) The asses of Kish, Saul's father, were lost. But they were too valuable to lose. "And Kish said to Saul, his son, 'Take now one of the servants with thee, and arise, go seek the asses.'"

But when they left home they little realized how far their search would lead them. "And he passed through the hill country of Ephraim, and passed through the land of Shalishah, but they found them not; then they passed through the land of Shalim, and there they were not; and he passed through the land of the Benjamites, but they found them not." Three days were consumed in this fruitless search, in stopping every traveler, asking many questions, scrutinizing every trail—but all to no purpose.

Lost she-asses! Well, what of them! Let them stray! Yes, but they are worth seeking, not for their worth only, but because the man who tracks them will presently come on a kingdom! Be faithful in a little and God will promote you to be faithful in much. Do what you have to do for God, and He will call you for the highest service! Often the finding of the hid treasure depends on the care with which we drive the plow of lowly labor along the common furrow of daily toil.

(2) By God's providence, which some call chance, the seekers found themselves in the land of Joseph, and there the thought of his father's possible anxiety arrested the steps of the young farmer, and he said, "Come, and let us return, lest my father leave caring for the asses, and take thought for us." This remark indicated a good and commendable trait in Saul's character. On the whole, a man who cares for the feelings of those nearest to him in the ties of natural kindred is likeliest to be a good ruler of men. Would that all our young men and women, especially those who are away from home in our great cities, would be a little more considerate of the heartstrings stretched even to breaking, and the eyes that often brim with tears because the tidings of their welfare are so scanty and intermittent! Saul feared the effect of three days on his father. What would he have thought of three weeks or months without tidings?

(3) Having arranged for the offering of the piece of shekel (a small silver coin), which was discovered in the bottom of the servant's pocket, as their gift to the seer, the two men headed for the gate of the little city "which was set on a hill," its white houses glistening in the intense sunshine. The maidens of whom they made inquiries, the fact that Samuel was in the city and on his way to a feast at the high place, the encounter with Samuel himself in the main street, and the tidings that the asses were found, were like so many signposts that pointed them in the way which they should go until they came to the place that awaited them— the seat and portion which had been prepared by the instructions of the prophet.

How evidently a divine hand was in all these circumstances! They could not have happened by chance. Clearly every separate detail had been planned by a designing mind with the express purpose of driving Saul into the precise position where he might stand still and hear the word of the Lord.

But if it was so with these circumstances, must we not believe that as much may be said of all circumstances? If a hair cannot fall to the ground from our head, or a sparrow from the tree, apart from God, can we say of anything that it is too trivial to come into the divine plan? Even let it be granted that many incidents happen at the instigation of evil men, yet they are permitted to reach us by the will of God, and therefore we may as much trace God's will in them for our own discipline and ennoblement as in those others which are evidently of His direct sending. God's purpose ran through the wicked deeds of the betrayers and murderers of our Lord. There was not a single event in all those fateful days that was not marked on the chart of divine providence; and since God is everywhere the same, and the same infinitely—so that we cannot say that He was more present there than here, or was more powerful then than now—we must admit that He is still as much in every circumstance of our lot as on those memorable and awful days when creation herself beheld the scenes of Gethsemane and Calvary with evident emotion.

Let it never be forgotten that straying asses, an unexpected encounter on the street, the presence of a coin in the pocket, or its absence, are all part of a divine plan. He who has open eyes may read the Father's handwriting and take the direction of His path as though angels had flashed before his eyes to direct him. And the prepared path always leads to the vacant seat and the waiting portion. The road may be long and the tax on patience and strength considerable, but the Father never draws His trustful and obedient child into a quagmire or leads him out on the moorland to perish of exposure to the cold. There is always a destination to which the road leads, and it only calls for the quick eye, the ready ear, and the obedient heart, to detect the things that God has prepared for those who love him.

II. The Incident of Saul's First Anointing.—Saul slept at Samuel's house that night, and on the housetop. The prophet had prepared his couch there with a special purpose which burned like a clear flame in his heart—for when the house was quiet, he stole up to the young man who was pondering the strange events of the day and "communed with Saul on the housetop."

He longed to stir Saul's soul to a profound sympathy with his own passionate and patriotic longings. He may have poured into the listening ear the story of his hopes and fears—of hopes that had been frustrated, of fears that seemed on the point of being realized. Probably he told the story of his own rejection because of the failure of his sons. He may have whispered into those young ears his longing that someone might appear at this juncture who would gather up the frayed and tangled threads and work out the divine pattern. Thus, with careful skill, Samuel awoke the sleeping soul of the young son of the soil who probably had lived in a narrow, circumscribed sphere, interested in flocks and herds, in vines and crops, in the talk of the countryside, but stirred with few thoughts of the national welfare.

He was awakened by Samuel before the breath that announced the dawn had stirred the leaves of the sleeping woods. "Samuel called to Saul on the housetop, saying, 'Up, that I may send thee on thy way.'" Then, near the descent at the edge of the city, the servant was sent on, and as the two men stood together Samuel took from out of his breast a flask of oil and poured it upon the strong young head bent beneath his touch, giving him the anointing which designated him as the king, and kissed him in token of his own fealty. "Is it not," said he, "that the Lord hath anointed thee to be prince over His inheritance?"

It was a great hour in Saul's life. No wonder that when he turned to leave Samuel it was with "*another heart*." The chronicle does not say that he received a *new heart*—there was no saving regeneration or conversion, no such radical change as comes over the soul at the hour of the new birth, or he would never have perished, as he did, on the field of Gilboa. But he had new aims, new conceptions of the importance and significance of life, new determinations and resolves. In a sense, though not the deepest, old things had passed away and everything had become new.

Let us mark this distinction. It is possible to have *another* but not a *new* heart—to be arrested by some stronger mind and inspired by a fresh ideal; but beneath the rapid sprouting of the seed there may be a slab of impenetrable and unchangeable rock. The work has been only on the surface, for the dew has sped before the sun and the cloud which seemed to presage rain has dissolved again in the sky. See that you make certain that your work is for eternity.

III. THE CIRCUMSTANCES THAT FOLLOWED.—When we are on God's path, we may certainly count on the corroboration of outward circumstances. If, in traveling by railway, one questions whether one is on the right track, it is a comfort to consult the timetables to see if the names of the stations, as we hurry through them, are those which are mentioned in the list. So, when questions arise—as they will when we are confronted by difficulties and obstacles—of whether we are in the line of God's will, it is an immense reassurance to meet with corroborating circumstances which tell us that we were right. Is not this what is meant by the words, "I will make my mountains a way?"

It was not enough that Peter should hear a voice speaking to his heart or see the sheet let down from heaven—he must hear the knock of the three men, sent from Cornelius, as they stand at the door of the tanner's house, inquiring for him (Acts 10). In all great decisions, seek the corroboration of circumstances. We will trace this in the subsequent chapter.

11

AS OCCASION SERVES

(1 Samuel 10:7)

"There lies no desert in the land of Life;
For e'en that tract that barrenest doth seem,
Labored of thee in faith and hope, shall teem
With heavenly harvests, and rich gatherings ripe."

KEBLE

CIRCUMSTANCES led up to Samuel's secret designation of Saul as king; and circumstances, so special and significant as to carry on their brow the divine impression, were destined to corroborate the momentous act. With unerring accuracy the old prophet anticipated them, and with unfailing precision each of them took place. "All those signs came to pass that day."

(1) First, by Rachel's tomb, near the border of Benjamin, two men met him to say that the asses had been found, and that his father had stopped thinking about the asses and was concerned for his son, saying, "What shall I do about my son?" This was a very significant evidence of the divine will and choice. It indicated that he was to be henceforth relieved of the care of the farm and the field, to devote himself to other and higher work. Asses could be found without his interposition. Others could attend to them and their like, but for him the kingdom was waiting, and the hearts of men were being prepared. The home ties, the

love of father and family, would always have a claim, but he must leave to others the care of the estates at Gibeah.

This sign is still of inestimable value to those who feel called to give themselves wholly to direct service for God. If it be the case that they are needed at home, to provide for the maintenance of aged parents or sisters, of wife or child, they have no right to withdraw from that sacred duty—that holy obligation—until God gives them an honorable discharge. The message to all such most certainly is that which the apostle gave in a time of great unsettlement to the Corinthian disciples. "Let each man abide in that calling wherein he was called." "Brethren, let each man, wherein he was called, therein abide with God" (1 Cor. 7:20, 24).

When God has given a call as clear and unmistakable as that which Saul received at the lips of Samuel, let the recipient wait trustfully and patiently for His hand to slacken the hold of circumstances. Without long delay the shore rope will be loosed, and the message will come in one form or another: "The asses are found." Any circumstance of that kind will be an unmistakable assurance that the Lord's voice has been speaking to the heart, and that His cloud is beckoning us to follow.

(2) Next, as he went forward, filled with bewilderment and awe, near the oak (or terebinth) of Tabor (the situation of which is absolutely unknown), Saul met three men going on a sacred pilgrimage to Bethel, which, from the days of Abraham and Jacob, had been hallowed by the most sacred associations.

These men were carrying, as Samuel said they would, their votive offerings to the shrine—three kids, three loaves and a bottle (or skin, *margin*) of wine. First they saluted him with the invariable Eastern greeting, "Peace be unto thee"; and presented him with two of the loaves, as though obeying an inner conviction which was pressed home on them by the Divine Spirit that he whom they had encountered was no ordinary wayfarer but one who might share their homage even with Almighty God.

What significance lay hid in this act also! Did it not imply that God would compel the respect and reverence of the nation to arise towards the king whom He had chosen, and that there should be no lack of the supplies which were required to sustain his royal state? Was it not an assurance that he need not be anxious about what he should eat or drink or how he should be clothed, since, if he sought first the kingdom of God and His righteousness, all things besides would certainly be added?

This, too, will befall each servant of God who steps out on the path of obedience. He may be leaving a well-established business and giving up some lucrative source of income; he may seem to be stepping from the boat onto the heaving, changeful waters; he may be blamed, as Moses was no doubt blamed, for casting himself and those dependent on him onto the trackless, inhospitable desert—but if he will be only true to God's call he will have no reason to repent. His bread shall be given him and his water shall be sure, the manna will fall where the cloud broods overhead; first the ravens, then the widow woman, and then the angels, will be commanded to provide bread that he may eat. God will care for his body in life, and in death will bury it with His own hands, as in the case of Moses, or by the hands of devout men, as when Stephen was carried to his grave amid great lamentations.

On one occasion in the Lord's life He gave a memorable lesson on this matter to His apostles. The tax collector had come to Peter with a demand which Peter could not meet, and he came to the Master with it. Doubtless, if the fisherman had still been plying his craft, there would have been no need for anxiety—out of the produce of his labor he would have been well able to meet the application; but, as it was, there was no money in his purse or house available for the purpose. "Go thou to the sea," said the Master, "and cast a hook, and take up the fish that first cometh up; and when thou hast opened his mouth, thou shalt find a shekel; that take and give them for Me and thee." It was in obedience to the Saviour's call that Peter had given up his own means of liveli-hood, and the Lord recognized that the responsibility of provid-ing for the needs that would otherwise have been met by his toil was incumbent on Himself. He identified Himself in the com-mon need when He said, *"for Me and thee."* If you go forth on Christ's errands, He will not be unrighteous to forget; you may surely trust Him to pay the taxes and all other legitimate dues. Do not set your hope on "the uncertainty of riches," or on the doles of the wealthy, but on God who giveth us richly all things to enjoy.

(3) Finally, Saul came to Gibeah (R.V. margin). The A.V. and R.V. note that there was a garrison of Philistines there, but other commentators, thinking it unlikely that Samuel would announce to Saul a fact which must have been so well-known to him, have preferred to employ the other meaning of the word translated *garrison*, and have rendered the sentence, "where the erection, col-umn, or monument, of the Philistines stands," probably reared by them to commemorate some famous victory.

Hard by this spot, and almost within sight of his home, Saul encountered a band of young men connected with the prophetic school which Samuel had established. They were coming down from the high place with a psaltery, a timbrel, a pipe and a harp. The afflatus of prophetic fervor and ecstasy was upon them, and as Saul beheld their holy rapture he fell under its spell. So great a change had passed over him during his brief absence from his home that he had now a sympathy with these divine raptures which he had never known before. Chords within his soul which had never vibrated before, began to answer in strange unison. Yearn-ings after God, susceptibility to spiritual impressions, the sense of the unseen and eternal, filled his soul. "The Spirit of God came mightily upon him, and he prophesied among them."

This remarkable assertion need not astonish us. It is by no means uncommon to find men temporarily and spasmodically affected by strong religious impressions, who are not permanently and savingly delivered from their former worldly or selfish manner of life. It is possible to be enlightened, to taste of the heavenly gift, to be a partaker of the Holy Ghost, to be solemnized by the powers of the world to come, and yet fall away. A land may have drunk of the rain and been moistened with the gentle dew, and yet bear thorns and thistles. Seed may spring up quickly where there is no depth of earth, and yet wither away. Simon Magus was deeply affected by all he saw and felt during Philip's visit to Samaria, but the apostle declared that he was still "in the gall of bitterness and the bond of iniquity."

But what to Saul was only a transient and superficial influence may become, in each of us, a permanent possession. The Spirit of God may come on us to fill us, and abide, as He did with those on whom He came in the early days of the Church. In successive waves of power and grace He may come on us, so that we may not only be filled suddenly and mightily for special work but be constantly sensible of the holy infillings as were the first converts in the highlands of Asia Minor, so that we may be permanently full as was Stephen. (Compare Acts 4:8; 13:52; 6:5; *note the change of tenses, etc.*)

Whenever God calls us to special service He provides a special anointing of the Holy Spirit. Remember how the Lord spoke unto Moses, saying, "See, I have called by name Bezaleel the son of Uri; and I have filled him with the Spirit of God, in wisdom, and in understanding, and in knowledge, and in all manner of workmanship." This is universally true. As certainly as there is the call, there will be the equipment. But we must look up for it, we must claim and appropriate it; without feeling it, we must reckon that it is ours, and step out on the predestined path. It is in the act of obedience that we become suddenly and thankfully aware of the possession. Oh, that the Spirit of Christ may come mightily on all His servants, so that they may be equipped for the demands of the present age, and that the Master may say of each of them,

"Behold My servant, whom I uphold; My chosen, in whom My soul delighteth. I have put My Spirit upon him, and he shall bring forth judgment to the people."

This transformation in the young farmer amazed all who knew him beforetime; and they said one to another, "What is this that has come upon the son of Kish? Is Saul also among the prophets?" It created as great a stir as when Saul of Tarsus joined the Christians, whom he had persecuted, or when Bunyan and Newton became ministers of the Word. One of the older people, however, divined the reason. Rumors of Saul's interview with Samuel were beginning to circulate, and he said, in effect: "Has he not been with Samuel, the father of these blessed and exalted movements? What wonder, then, if he partakes of his gifts!"

When the first tremor of excitement had passed, and Saul regained full mastery of himself, he went up to the high place, probably for quiet meditation and prayer, that he might comprehend the full significance of the crowding events which had transpired within the recent hours. To whom can we turn, most Holy God, in the supreme moments of life, but unto Thee? Only Thou canst understand.

Ere Samuel dismissed his astonished and awe-stricken guest, he bade him act in each circumstance as occasion served (v. 7). There is always room for the exercise of sanctified common sense. The circumstances may be divinely contrived, but we must use them for good or evil, making them steppingstones or stumblingblocks. The same circumstances may come to all, but one man receives their lesson and transmits his answer in a very different spirit from his friend and neighbor. In one case the sun and shower produce flowers and grain, in another weeds and poppies. The divine guidance of our lives does not obviate the necessity for the exercise of prudence that looks before and after *and upwards* in order to ascertain what the will of the Lord is.

There is always in the regimen of life an abundant need for the exercise of our judgment, through which the light of God may be shining as through a clear pane of glass. We are not dumb, driven cattle, nor the creatures of fate or chance. We are not automatons. So long as we look for guidance it will be freely given, but when it is given, we must use it, and it is useless unless we do. Only they that *receive* the abundance of grace, and the gift of righteousness, shall reign in life.

On that memorable night when God's angel achieved the deliverance of Peter from his prison, we are told that the celestial visitant led the dazed apostle through the first and second streets, and then departed from him; and when Peter *had considered the thing* he went to the house of Mary. As long as he was bewildered and half asleep, living in a trance, walking in dreamland, it was necessary that he should be carefully watched and led; but as soon as the sharp morning air had revived him and brought him to himself, so that he was able to consider the matter, he was left to act on the decisions of his own sanctified common sense.

To him that overcometh, the Master promises to give a white stone, which is surely the Urim and Thummim stone—a judgment through which the Shekinah light glows and shines. May it be our happy privilege to receive it at His hands, that we may be able to say with our Lord, "My judgment is just, because I seek not my own will, but His that sent me."

12

THE INNER AND OUTER CONFLICTS

(1 Samuel 11)

"What if He hath decreed that I shall first
Be try'd in humble state and things adverse,
By tribulations, injuries, insults,
Contempts, and scorns, and snares, and violence!"

MILTON

THE eleventh verse records a great victory. It was the first public act of the reign of Saul, taking place a month after his inauguration. It at once justified his selection and silenced the voice of detraction; he stood forth before the eyes of his own people, and of surrounding nations, as every inch a man and a king.

But in this chapter, for eyes that look beneath the surface, there is the record of another fight. There was the outward fight that Saul made for Israel; there was the inner and previous fight that Saul made for himself, against himself; and it was because he had conquered in the latter, of which there was probably no symptom or sign to the outward eye, that he carried himself erect in the fight with Nahash the Ammonite.

This is always so; within the fight there is another fight. Within the fight that men are waging with the sin and darkness of the world there is always the inner fight, which they must wage with themselves and for themselves. If, to use the suggestion of another, you had been familiar with Howard, the great prison evangelist, or had known Clarkson, who delivered the slave; if you had been permitted to read the secrets of the heart of Garrison, the great American philanthropist, you would have known that, full often, each was sick and weary with the inward combat, and closed the door of his heart upon the outward fight that he might turn his thought and attention to himself; and you would have heard the soldier of Christ saying bitterly to himself: "It would be easy for me to conquer, and to win the battle for my Lord against these outward ills, if only I had not perpetually to wage this inward fight; if only I had solid ground to stand on, instead of the shifting sand of my own vacillating nature and irresolute temper." Perhaps you might even have heard these great soldiers saying: "Surely it would be better to relinquish the outward conflict, so as to bend all attention to the control of my inner tendencies."

Yet it is good for us all that these two conflicts should go on side by side, for if a man were only conflicting against the evil of the world and knew nothing about the inward fight, he might become arrogant and suppose that he stood aloof from the common sin and the common temptation; and, on the other hand, if we were only to confine ourselves to the inward conflict, we might grow morbid and self-centered, dispirited and depressed.

No, let those two go on together, and let the victories that we win for God in the outward field of vision be weighed against the awful consciousness of failure that we all carry in our inner experience. Let these two go on side by side, and let every man know that if he conquers within he will conquer without, and that if he fails within he will fail without. It is just in proportion as we are able to overcome, as Saul did, in his heart, that we shall overcome, as he did, against the Ammonites.

Two thoughts lie upon this chapter which are full of interest—first, Saul's inward fight and conquest; secondly, Saul's outward fight and conquest.

I. SAUL'S INWARD FIGHT, CONFLICT AND VICTORY.—(1) *He fought the subtle temptation to pride.* Samuel, eager to constitute the new kingdom, called a great national assembly at Mizpeh, where so great a defeat and victory had been recorded in earlier days. In their teeming multitudes the Israelites gathered there and proceeded to elect their king by an appeal to God through a lot. After prayer the lot was cast, and the disposing of it was left to God. First the tribe of Benjamin was taken, then the clan of the Matrites, then the family of Kish, and ultimately the lot indicated Saul, the son of Kish, but he was not to be found. He knew from his previous conversation with Samuel that he was God's designated king; that the anointing oil had flowed over his head; that he was possessed of a kingly presence, standing head and shoulders above all ordinary men. If ever a man might have stood to the front and allowed ambition to master him, that was the moment when Saul might have stood forth and presented himself to his people as the unrivaled candidate for their allegiance and the crown. However, he was not to be found. They looked for him everywhere in vain. And it was only when, for the second time, they appealed to the direction of the Urim and Thummim, that he was discovered— hiding among the baggage wagons.

This modesty was extremely beautiful, and our admiration of the natural traits of Saul's character cannot but be greatly enhanced by his unobtrusiveness. It reminds one of Athanasius, who left the city of Alexandria that he might not be elected bishop, and of Ambrose, who more than once sought to evade the responsibility which was thrust upon him at Milan. It reminds us also of John Livingstone, who, when he was chosen to preach that famous sermon of Kirk o' Shotts, traveled as quickly as possible in another direction, and only after some hours was led by the Spirit of God to turn again and assume the blessed burden. Those that assume to themselves high positions, yielding before the proud spirit of self-assumption, fail; but they who humble themselves, who generally think others better than they are, who deprecate notoriety and show, are such as God exalts.

(2) *There was the strong temptation which assailed him to vindictiveness.* Amid the shouts, "God save the King," which applauded his nomination there were the voices of detractors, men of Belial, who whispered, "How shall this man save us?" One such voice is enough to spoil all the adulation that may be strewn before us by the crowd. What public man is there who has not felt that the clamor of kind voices was marred by the one sentence of criticism and spite, so that the drop of vinegar turned all the rest acid? These voices must have stung the heart of Saul. The adder's poison must have penetrated to his heart; but he quenched the desire for revenge; conquered, and trampled beneath his feet the smoldering embers of vindictiveness. It was not that he was pusillanimous, for we are told, in this same chapter, that when he heard of the cry of Jabesh-gilead "his anger was greatly kindled." He was capable of flaming forth against wrong, but in this case he held himself well in hand. To use the old English phrase of the A.V., *He held his peace.* The more one examines that phrase, the more fascinating it is— to hold your peace, not to let it go, not to let it be taken or snatched from you, not to let it be trampled under foot in anger, but to hold to it in the midst of irritation and fret, to hold your ground. "He held his peace."

The Hebrew, as suggested by the margin in the R.V., is still more striking. "He was as though he had been deaf"—he pretended not to hear. He did hear; every word had struck deep into his soul, but he made as though he were deaf. It is a great power when a man can act as though he were deaf to slander, deaf to detraction, deaf to unkind and uncharitable speeches, and treat them as though they had not been spoken, turning from man to God, leaving with God his vindication, believing that God sooner or later will give him a chance, as He most certainly gave Saul a chance, of vindicating the true prowess and temper of his soul.

If Saul had listened to these men and noticed them, he might have drifted into an awkward and perplexing position, for if, on the one hand, he had passed over their slander, he might have laid himself open to the imputation of cowardice; whereas if, on the other, he had noticed it, he might have been goaded to act tyrannically, and so as to alienate a large number of his people. He could not have done better than to act as though he were deaf, and to conquer the spirit of vindictive revenge by the spirit of self-restraint.

(3) *There was one more temptation by which he must have been plied, the temptation to ostentation.* When the assemblage was dispersed he returned from Mizpeh to Gibeah. He had been designated by Samuel, and kissed by him in token of homage. Sign after sign had indicated him to be God's choice for Israel; he had stood forth amid the people's clamor, the acknowledged king of the land; a number of young men, whose hearts were fired by loyal enthusiasm, had thronged about his path, and with songs of rejoicing had accompanied him to his home; he was conscious of being able to rally about him the chivalry and strength of his fatherland; and yet, when he was back again in Gibeah, in spite of every temptation to ostentation and excess, he was noble enough to return to his rustic life; he took again in hand his plow, and for one whole month he drove the oxen across the fields, meditating much on the strange chance which had befallen, and wondering when God would open the door for him to step forth into the manifestation and enjoyment of the royalty which was already his.

These were the elements of a truly great soul. We do not forget Gilboa; the frenzied insanity by which his career was afterwards blasted; how more than once or twice he hurled his javelin at David; that he became moody and morose; that he betrayed the heart of a murderer and died the death of a suicide; but at this time of his life at least, in his young manhood, he put his foot upon pride and remained humble; he put his foot upon the spirit of revenge and left it with God to vindicate him; put his foot upon that love of ostentation that tempts us all, setting himself to do his daily work, and waiting until God summoned him to take the helm of the state. We cannot but admire this greatly.

You, too, may be conscious of the presence of many amiable natural traits, but unless the natural virtues of your soul be possessed and strengthened by the power of the Holy Ghost they will not be able ultimately to withstand the awful conflict of the world. See to it that in and through the traits of your own amiable nature there may come the transcendent life of the ever-glorious Saviour, that your character may not be the wild growth of nature but the established and permanent indwelling of the Son of God by the Holy Spirit.

II. THE OUTWARD CONFLICT.—One evening as Saul came back from the field he heard that low wail of distress and panic by which the Eastern populace makes known its anguish; and as he drew near to Gibeah he asked what it meant. "What aileth the people that they weep?" Then the story was told how, across the Jordan, in the land of Gilead, the city of Jabesh-gilead was hard pressed by the Ammonites, who, a hundred years before, had been disastrously defeated by Jephthah, but who had never relinquished their claim to the land. Under Nahash, the king, they had gathered in overwhelming numbers around the beleaguered city. Its citizens had tried their best to extricate themselves, but in vain. One week of respite alone had been extracted from the contemptuous clemency of Nahash; and if at the end of that week no deliverance came, then the right eye of every man would be put out, which, of course, would make him useless for purposes of war, because in battle the left eye was always covered by the shield.

In despair the messengers came to Gibeah of Benjamin, because in the days of the judges Jabesh-gilead had refused to join in the war of extermination against the Benjamites, and had given forty of its daughters in marriage to their sons. There was, therefore, a blood-tie between the people of Jabesh-gilead and those of Gibeah, and in this awful hour they felt they had a claim for help—if they would not help, who would? But the people of Gibeah despaired. It seemed as if it were impossible in that short space to send effectual help. Saul was living in the midst of them, but they had no hope that he could help them. The day threatened to close in hopeless despondency and despair.

Then the man who had conquered himself became suddenly aware of the uprising of an altogether new power in his heart. We are told that "the Spirit of God came mightily upon Saul"; a little further on we learn that "the fear of the Lord fell on the people"; and still further on, "the Lord wrought a great salvation for Israel."

If you will be true in the inward battle, if by the grace of God you will trample upon the sins which so easily beset you, the time will come in your life also when the Spirit of God will come upon you with an almost overwhelming power and bear you forward to do what otherwise would be absolutely impossible; and as He works on you, He will work also on the people and on the foe.

Instantly Saul laid hold of his bullocks, slew them, cut them in pieces, and by messengers sent those pieces throughout the land. In some such way, as Sir Walter Scott tells us, the old Highland chieftain used to summon the clans for war by the mission of the fiery cross. Killing an animal, kindling a fire, the cross was scorched in the flames, which were quenched in blood, and it was sent throughout the land, and every man who saw it was bound to hasten to the field.

Similarly, the entire people throughout the whole land of Israel obeyed the royal summons. Three hundred thousand Israelites and thirty thousand of Judah rallied "after Saul and after Samuel." They were at first but an undisciplined mob. Probably they were armed with scythes and goads, for the Philistines had deprived them of all other weapons; but Saul, in the power of God, numbered them—i.e., disciplined, arranged and marshalled them; directing them by three different routes to fall upon the Ammonites in the morning. A message was sent to Jabesh-gilead to tell the people that help was coming, and their hearts were glad. Then, as the morning broke over the quiet hills and valleys of Gilead, and the little city was astir with expectation and hope, from three different sides Saul launched his army upon the sleeping hosts. Panic-stricken, they sprang to their feet; hardly awake, and dazed with the clamor of the battle cries, they were unable to resist the onset of the men of Israel; and the rout was so complete that, by the noontide, two men were not left together. It was a wonderful victory and an auspicious beginning for the new reign.

Would you not win such a victory over the sin of the world? If so, there must be self-mastery. Gird yourselves to fight "the good fight of faith." We are reminded that there are several circles to that fight. First, there is, of course, *the outer circle of circumstances.* A man must always begin with these, and rightly so. It is quite wise on your part to give up that business which is a constant source of temptation; to remove from that house where bad people live; to renounce that literature, those books and that recreation which are constantly causing you to offend; to extricate yourself from that friendship or fellowship which has been your curse. That is the first thing to do. Get right with your circumstances; touch not, taste not, handle not; come out and be separate. At any cost deliver yourself from the conditions of life that tempt you to sin.

Second, there is *the inner circle of habit,* for if our circumstances are like our clothes, our habits are like our skin, and every man has got to fight his lonely fight against habit; it may be of alcoholism; it may be of narcotism; it may be of impurity and immorality; nothing but the power of God can break the bonds that bind you. That is the second great fight in a man's life.

Third, there is *the battle against heredity.* It may be that your father was a passionate man and has passed on, perhaps from his ancestors, strong and vehement desires; that your mother was a vain, or proud, or quick-tempered woman, and that she has passed on to you something of her own quick, sensitive nature; that you cannot keep calm and still, cannot hold your peace, cannot seem as if you were deaf. Everyone has to meet with a certain number of predispositions in his life, which he has inherited, and which make the battle harder. Enumerate them, consider them, know them; then in the name of God put the grave of Christ between you and them, and let them meet you only through Him that died. Die to them all, die to the first Adam, die to yourself because you have risen to the second. In acting thus you may break the entail and arrest for others that awful inheritance into which you have come.

Then, after all, when all this is said and done, when your outward circumstances are adjusted, when by the grace of God you have broken the spell of habit, when you have died to heredity, then you come face to face with *the inner citadel of yourself.* There are things that you must not do, temptations to which you must not yield, an inner self which you must crucify. Ah, that lonely fight! Ah, the flowers and grass that become trampled down in the wrestle while the blood of your heart is sprinkled on the sward, and you know that all the possessions of your outward life are as nothing to you compared to the agony of the inward conflict. What is success? What is applause? What is the crown of victory compared with your confessed failure to yourself? Thus we fight our fight, and win in the power of the loving Christ. And then Ammon, Ammon, Ammon! Ah, not two men are left together. Fight, fight, fight the good fight of faith; lay hold upon the life which is life indeed.

13

FORSAKEN? NEVER!

(1 Samuel 12:22)

" For the glory and the passion of this midnight
I praise Thy name, I give Thee thanks, O Christ!
Thou that hast neither failed me nor forsaken
Through these hard hours with victory overpriced.
Now that I too of Thy passion have partaken,
For the world's sake—called—elected—sacrificed!"

H. HAMILTON KING

WHILE the whole land was ringing with the news of Saul's exploit in the deliverance of Jabesh-gilead, it appeared to Samuel to be an auspicious moment for confirming the kingdom in his hand: and therefore he summoned a great convocation of the nation at Gilgal.

On that spot Israel had encamped for the first night after crossing the Jordan, and the twelve great stones commemorating that event were still visible. There the act of circumcision had been performed, cleansing the people of the neglect of the wilderness; and there, too, the first Passover in the Land of Promise had been celebrated. Amid these great memorials and memories of the past, with the swiftly flowing river sweeping constantly beside them to the Dead Sea, surrounded by all the associations of those glorious days, which had left an unfading splendor upon the history of their fathers, the people gathered from far and near to crown Saul king. He had been designated at Mizpeh; he was to be crowned at Gilgal; it was the inauguration of his reign, its ratification and confirmation by the entire people. After this great ceremony had taken place, Saul and his people rejoiced together with peace offerings and thank offerings before God; and this was the moment that Samuel chose to lay down his office as judge—the last of the judges, and the first of the prophets.

I. SAMUEL'S RESIGNATION.—An end must come to the longest and most successful ministry, and the author of the book of Ecclesiasticus, reverting to this event in Samuel's life, says: "Before his long sleep Samuel made protestation of his innocence, before God and the people." Yes, the long sleep will come to all, and happy are they who before they lay their heads down to the last sleep and their spirits enter to receive their final award, are able to extend their hands and bare their hearts before those who have known them best, and say, "These at least are clean."

This is what Samuel by the grace of God was able to do. Standing bareheaded before the vast audience of the men of Israel, and pointing to his white locks, he said, "I am old and gray-headed, and I have walked before you [as in Eastern lands a shepherd precedes his flock] from my boyhood up." His had been an unblemished career, and for his own sake and for the sake of God on whose behalf he stood, he was anxious to obtain from the people a vindication of the blamelessness of his career. He therefore protested: "I have not defrauded you, nor oppressed you. Whose ox have I taken? Whose ass? Can any man confront me as having taken from his hand even a sandal as a bribe that I should turn away mine eyes from his misdoing?" And all the people, like the leaves of the forest rustling before the wind, with one unanimous consent, cried: "Thou hast not defrauded, nor oppressed, nor taken anything from our hand."

But the old man was not content; he wanted to bind the people by a solemn oath, as in the very sight of God and the king; and, therefore, he said, lifting his hand to heaven, "I call God to witness against you this day and His anointed king, that what you have said is true." And again, from the lips of all the people, with one unanimous shout, there came the response, "God is witness." The old man was comforted, and added: "Yes, God is witness, the very God who brought our people out of Egypt, and appointed Moses and Aaron."

Oh, that all our public men today were as clean-handed and pure-hearted as Samuel was!—that when the records of their actions are rehearsed before the judgment seat of God it may be discovered that those who have been high in office have not prostituted their high position for their own emolument, or acted for private gain, but that they are clean-handed and pure-hearted. Happy is that nation whose public men are free from all complicity with bribery and from making profit out of the necessities or the sore distress of their fatherland!

II. He Designated His People's Sin.—It was a great opportunity to show them where they had done wrong, and a man whose own hands are clean is permitted to be the sincere critic of others' misdoing. See to it that your own eye is single, and that the beam is extracted from it before you essay to remove the mote from your brother's eye. In several particulars he pleaded with that dense mass of people, and dared to hold up the crimes of his nation, that they might see them as they were.

First, he set himself to show the difference between their former and their latter method of procedure. He carried their thoughts back to Egypt, and, in effect, said: "When your fathers were in bondage to the Egyptians, and under the oppression of Pharaoh, you cried unto Jehovah, and in gracious answer He raised up deliverance. And when in the days of the judges you were oppressed first by Sisera, then by the Philistines, and then by the people of Moab, you cried to God for deliverance, and it came; but now, when the threatened invasion of Nahash, the king of the Ammonites, was filling the horizon with thunderclouds, instead of holding a great invocation for prayer, you insisted upon my appointing a king. Why have you deteriorated? Why was prayer your natural resort three hundred years ago and now it is neglected? Is it not because you are prayerless that you have drifted from your ancient moorings? In this is a great sin."

Must not we always take care that, instead of saying impulsively and impetuously, "We will do this or that," we should constantly wait before God that He would appoint a deliverer?

Second, in his dealing with the people, he put a new reading upon past history. On their side, they pointed out the successive catastrophes which had befallen their country; how the Ammonites, the Philistines, the Moabites, and Sisera, and other surrounding nations, had oppressed them and brought them under their power, and therefore, as a way of deliverance from such troubles, they had argued the necessity of having a king. Samuel, of course, admitted the successive afflictions which had befallen his people, but he did not put the same reading upon them. He said: "You demand a king who shall make such catastrophes no longer possible, but I tell you, on the other hand, that whether you have a king or not, if you forget God, as you *have* forgotten Him, and if you turn to Baalim and Ashtaroth, as you *have* turned to them, neither your king, nor any alternative mode of government you can invent, will deliver you from the consequences." In other words, he made it clear that it was not the presence or absence of a monarchy, but the lack of singleness of purpose and devotion to Jehovah which had been the cause and root of all their troubles.

Again, there is a lesson for ourselves. After all, it is not this man or that who is necessary to a church, so long as the church itself is living before God in incorruption and sincerity of truth, and is following the lead of the beacon fire by night and the cloudy pillar by day. When a church is right with God, God stands for the church.

Third, he indicated to the people that God had never failed to send them a man when a man was needed. He said: "Look back upon your past history. Even apart from a hereditary line of kings with the prestige of royal descent, God has always raised up a man to help you in an emergency. Consider—did not He raise up Moses and Aaron? Did not He raise up Jephthah and Barak [see R.V. margin], Gideon and myself? See how perpetually, in the dark hour, in answer to prayer, God has sent you the man that was needed. Could you not have trusted Him; and instead of being so urgent for a king, could you not have waited for Him to do for you as He has done aforetime?"

Lastly, he said: "My countrymen, you have greatly deteriorated; you have failed in your faith. You have demanded a visible king and have forgotten the invisible Lord; you have magnified the arm of flesh and have forgotten the mighty power of the Eternal. You have been sheltering under the idea of a new royalty, whereas God was your King, your true head, the Leader and Patron of the nation. You should have rested only on Him."

Are we not all liable to the same lapse of faith? We look to the visible and forget the invisible. The air is filled with anxiety, clamor and controversy, while in the shadow, behind the thin veil of sense, stands the eternal-crowned Christ, waiting ever to trim the lamps of the golden lampstands and to hold the stars in His right hand. It was a brave thing, a noble thing, a right thing, for Samuel to show to his people how they had drifted from the old true standing ground of faith into practical atheism and unbelief.

III. SAMUEL'S ASSURANCE.—Having handed over his office to Saul, who henceforth was to be the shepherd and leader of the chosen people, and having dealt with their failure and deterioration, he went on to say with inimitable sweetness, "The Lord will not forsake His people for His great name's sake." Oh, take these words to heart, and let them sink, like a refrain of music, into your soul. The Lord will not forsake His people! They may have lost their ideal; for a moment they may have drifted from their ancient moorings of childlike confidence, but the Lord cannot forsake His people, for His great name's sake.

How perpetually this argument was used by the holy men of the old time. For instance, in Exodus 32:12, where God talks of casting away His people, when they had made the golden calf and worshiped it with garlands and dances, Moses dares to go into the Divine Presence and say: "Lord, Thou canst not do it, for if Thou dost, Thy character will be impugned, and the Egyptians will say, 'He was not able to bring them in; He brought them out, but His power was not sufficient to accomplish that to which He had put His hand.' Thou canst not do it. Thy credit is at stake!"

And in Joshua 7:9, when Israel had fled before the men of Ai, Joshua threw himself upon the ground before the ark and cried, "O my God, if Thy people fail like this, what will the Egyptians say? What will the Philistines say? What will the nations of Canaan say? And what wilt Thou do for Thy great name. Before heaven and earth Thou wilt stand discredited if Thou failest to give us this land as Thou hast promised."

Then in Isaiah 48:9, 11, later on in the history of the chosen people, Isaiah, dealing with their sins, and speaking to them in God's name, says: "For My name's sake will I defer Mine anger; and for My praise will I refrain for thee, that I cut thee not off." "For Mine own sake, for Mine own sake, will I do it; for how should My name be profaned? And My glory will I not give to another."

In Ezekiel 20, these remarkable words are repeated thrice: "I wrought for My name's sake, that it should not be profaned in the sight of the nations, among whom they were." God's name is God's character. He is bound by His self-respect not to forsake His people.

The old prophet went on to say: "It hath pleased the Lord to make you His people." God hides His reasons. He loves because He will. The flame of His love requires no fuel. The bush is not consumed for its maintenance. We may put alongside with these those words of the great apostle: "He gave Himself for us, that He might redeem us from all iniquity and purify unto Himself a people for His own possession." This assurance applies to men:

(1) *As Individuals*—God will not forsake you. He did not choose you because of your goodness or beauty, and He will not forsake you because you have failed of your best. He has made you His child by adoption and grace, not that there was anything in you to specially attract Him, but because He would. Someday He may explain to you His reason, but just now there is no reason that any of us can guess at—why we have been chosen from the rest of men to be His. *It has pleased Him* to make us His sons and daughters. We may have sinned against Him and grieved His Holy Spirit, we may have mixed ourselves with the seed of the people among whom we dwell, but God will not forsake His people. If He did, there would be a charge against *His love* that it was not infinite, that it ceased after sin had reached to a certain height of outrage, that it could not abound over sin. His *power* also would be impugned, for the lost spirits in hell would boast that He had attempted more than He was able to perform—that He had not counted the cost.

There would also be an imputation upon His *immutability*. It would be spread through the universe that He took up a sinful soul, cleansed and clothed it, loved and blessed it, and then He changed. At the news that God could be fickle, the palace of eternity would rock, the throne of heaven shake, and the mighty vault of space would reel to destruction. God dare not surrender the work which He has begun in the heart of man. That is why we may count on being saved. We have no positive claim on God;

there is no native beauty or attractiveness to Him who sees the inner life; there is nothing necessary in our service; but He has set His love upon us, and He must go through with it, and stand to His bargain before all worlds. O soul of man, God will not forsake thee.

(2) *As a Church* why could not God forsake Israel? Because the chosen people was the type of what He desired every nation to become; and therefore He must needs go on building up Israel, that His type might not be broken; and He had to work through Israel to bring other nations to its level. If God had abandoned Israel, how could He have hoped to regenerate the world?

What was true of Israel may be true of a church. There may be many failures and inconsistencies in her that ought to be altered. But God cannot cast her away in spite of all her sinful imperfection. He will refine and purify her till she realizes His ideal and becomes His perfect Bride.

(3) *As a Nation.*—Our country cannot go drifting on into materialism and irreligion, as she is doing. God cannot afford to let her become immoral and debased; cannot permit her to follow in the way of Rome and Greece; cannot forsake the people whom He has blessed and used since the days of Alfred, who have been the pioneers of missionary and Christian civilization through the entire world. For His name's sake He cannot do it. No, it is certain that, sooner or later, a great revival of religion will bring us back to our first love.

(4) *As a World.*—God cannot forsake this world, reeking though it be with blasphemy and impurity, with tyranny and sin. It has been saturated with the blood of His Son and of myriads of His saints. It has been bedewed with the tears of the noblest souls that have ever breathed, and it is yet destined to shine amidst its sister stars with an untarnished beauty; it is to be the specimen to all the universe of what God can do with a fallen world and a degraded race. God cannot forsake our earth, and some day we shall see

her glistening in the light that shone over Paradise, and enswathed with an unpolluted atmosphere. Purity shall breathe again over her landscapes and oceans. Yes, the children of men will come out from all the sin and evil by which they have been so long oppressed, and shall walk in the white robes of purity, love and truth. "The Lord will not forsake His people for His great name's sake, because it hath pleased the Lord to make you a people unto Himself."

14

NOT CEASING IN PRAYER

(1 Samuel 12:16–25)

"O, who can tell how many hearts are altars to His praise,
From which the silent prayer ascends through patient nights and days!
The sacrifice is offered still in secret and alone,
O world, ye do not know them, but He can help His own."

A. A. Procter

IN all Samuel's career there is nothing finer than the closing scene of his public action as the judge and leader of the Hebrew nation. Had he died young, his place in the annals of his country, and indeed in history, would have been much lower and our appreciation of his character much less. Naturally he found it difficult to step down from his premiership and inaugurate a regime with which he had no sympathy, since it seemed to be a setting aside of Israel's greatest glory in having God for King. But he suppressed his strong personal antipathies and did his very best to start the nation on the new path it had chosen, selecting a king with the utmost care, and, regardless of personal suffering, bridging over the gulf between the old order and the new.

We cannot turn from the record of the great convocation, assembled before the Lord at Gilgal to ratify Saul's election, without noticing the repeated allusions to Samuel's power in prayer. He appears to have been the John Knox of his age, as mighty in prayer as in statesmanship. His whole career seems to have been bathed in the spirit of supplication.

As a boy, with hands meekly clasped (as Sir Joshua Reynolds has depicted him), he asked God to speak, while his ear was quick and attent to catch His lowest whispers. In the book of Psalms he is mentioned as chief among those that call on God's name, and as having been answered (99:6). The prophet Jeremiah alludes to the wonderful power which he exercised in intercessory prayer when he pleaded for his people (15:1). All Israel knew the long, piercing cry of the prophet of the Lord. In their perils his intercessions had been their deliverance, and in their battles his prayers had secured them victory (1 Sam. 7:8, 8:6). There was "an open road" between God and him, so that thoughts of God's thinking were able to come into his heart; and he reflected them back again with intense and burning desire.

I. SAMUEL'S PRAYER FOR THUNDER AND RAIN.—The heart of man cries out for divine authentication. In every age a crooked and perverse generation seeks a sign, and in seeking it proves how far it has wandered from the source of light and become blinded in spiritual vision. If our nature realized its divine ideal, it would discern God in the ordinary and common incidents of providence, in the morning light and the summer air, in dews that noiselessly alight and zephyrs that gently kiss the slumbering woods, in the garniture of spring and the carpeting of flowers (Acts 14:17). But the eyes of the soul are blinded, and men do not see the traces of the divine footprints across the world day by day. "Lord," said the prophet, "Thy hand is lifted up, yet they see not" (Isa. 26:11, R.V.).

In default of the faculty of detecting God's presence in the noiseless and ordinary providence of life, man asks for some startling phenomena to prove that God is speaking. "Bring," he cries to the heaven-sent messenger, "credentials so startling and extraordinary that I may know without doubt that you are properly accredited. The still, small voice is not enough. We must have the hurricane, the fire, and the bolt from the blue. Then we shall know that God speaks by you and that the word from your lips is true."

Samuel knew this, and he perhaps longed for some divine corroboration of his words. God's trusted servants are content to work through long years amid persistent resistance and apathy, if only they are assured that they are on the line of the divine purpose. "And it came to pass at the time of the offering of the evening sacrifice that Elijah the prophet came near, and said, 'Lord God of Abraham, Isaac and of Israel, let it be known this day that Thou art God in Israel, and that I am Thy servant, and that I have done all these things at Thy word.'" Thus, in a supreme moment, one of the noblest of his successors appealed to God, and his words expressed what was in Samuel's heart at this great hour. He had surrendered his prerogatives and introduced his successor; had confronted his people with their sins and announced the heavy penalties that must follow on disobedience; and he yearned that they should hear another voice, asseverating his words and pressing them home on conscience and on heart.

It was under the influence of these thoughts that he concluded his address and appeal with the announcement, "Now, therefore, stand still, and see this great thing, which the Lord will do before your eyes. Is it not wheat harvest today? I will call unto the Lord, and He shall send thunder and rain, that ye may perceive and see that your wickedness is great which ye have done in the sight of the Lord, in asking you a king."

During the wheat harvest, lasting from the middle of May to the middle of June, rain is almost unknown in Palestine, and the occurrence of a thunderstorm, coming as it did at *the call* of the aged prophet, was too startlingly unusual to be viewed as other than the divine authentication of his claims.

It may be supposed that this incident is altogether without

parallel, belonging to the realms of Old Testament story; but I cannot think it to be so. Nature is much more sympathetic with man than we sometimes suppose, because her beauty or terror is but the veil beneath which the Almighty hides Himself. How, save on the supposition that God answered the appeal of His servants, can we account for the fact of the terrific tempest that swept over our shores when the proud Armada of Spain menaced the liberties of Protestant England? And how, save on the supposition that Heaven itself protested against the blasphemous pretensions of the Papacy, can we account for the memorable fact that on the afternoon when the dogma of the Papal Infallibility was announced, the Vatican at midday was suddenly invested with a pall of blackest midnight?

But there are other methods of divine authentication on which every true servant of God may rely. When Paul and Barnabas abode for a long time in Iconium, speaking boldly in the Lord, "He gave testimony unto the word of His grace"; and the writer of the Epistle to the Hebrews generalizes the experience of the early heralds of the gospel when he says that the message of God's great salvation was confirmed by them that heard the word, "God also bearing them witness, both with signs and wonders, and with divers miracles, and gifts of the Holy Ghost, according unto His own will" (Acts 14:3; Heb. 2:3–4).

We cannot be too thankful for the witness of the Holy Spirit, whose voice is to the faithful servant of God all, and more, that the thunder was to Samuel. It was this that armed the primitive saints with irresistible power. "We are His witnesses," cried the apostles, "and so is also the Holy Ghost, whom God hath given to them that obey Him." "Our gospel," wrote the greatest apostle of all, "came not unto you in word only, but also in power, and in the Holy Ghost, and in much assurance" (1 Thess. 1:5).

May I ask if my fellow servants realize this—that the Holy Spirit is in the Church today, that He is prepared to bear witness to every true word which is spoken in the name of Jesus, and that He will convict of sin, righteousness and judgment; so that the faith of our hearers should not stand in the wisdom of man but in the power of God, God bearing them witness and giving them the Holy Spirit (1 Cor. 2:1–4; Acts 15:8).

This is the fatal lack of our preaching. We speak earnestly and faithfully, but we do not sufficiently look for nor rely on the divine co-witness; we do not understand the communion and fellowship of the Comforter, and our hearers do not hear His voice thrilling their souls, as thunder in the natural world, with the conviction that the things which we speak are the truths of God. Only let the passionate longing of our heart be "Father, glorify Thy name," and voices will come as from heaven, saying, "I have both glorified it, and will glorify it again." While some that stand by may say that "It thundered," others will say "An angel spoke" (John 12:28–29).

Oh, our God, give us such power in prayer that when we pray Thou shalt answer "in the secret place of thunder," and send thunder and rain.

II. Samuel's Unceasing Intercessions.—Terrified by the loud thunder-peals and the torrents of rain, the people were urgent to secure Samuel's intercession on their behalf. They feared for their lives and their property, and entreated him to pray for them. "Pray for thy servants unto the Lord *thy* God," they said, "that we die not"; and the emphasis they laid on the word *thy* seemed to indicate that they felt no longer worthy of their ancient prerogative as the chosen people. Touched with their appeal, and confident that Jehovah only desired to corroborate his word, the aged seer calmed their fears, urged them never to turn aside to vain idols, which could neither profit nor deliver, assured them that the Lord would not forsake them, and ended with the striking words: *"Moreover, as for me, God forbid that I should sin against the Lord in ceasing to pray for you."*

Samuel realized that prayer was action in the spiritual plane. The energy which we exert in action in the physical sphere becomes prayer in the spiritual. It has often been said, *Laborare est orare* ("To labor is to pray"); but the converse is much truer, *Orare est laborare* ("To pray is to labor"). "The fervent prayer of a righteous man," says James, "availeth much in its working." Therefore it was that when the good Epaphras could no longer help his brethren at Colosse by his words and deeds, he betook himself to prayer and labored fervently for them all in prayer (Col. 4:12).

> *"Work shall be prayer, if all be wrought*
> *As Thou wouldst have it done:*
> *And prayer, by Thee inspired and taught,*
> *Itself with work be one."*

Samuel could no longer exert his energies for his people as he had done. The limitations imposed by his advancing years, and by the substitution of the kingdom for his judgeship, made it impossible that he should make his yearly rounds as aforetime, but he was able to translate all that energy into another method of helpfulness. The light became heat, the water became steam. The prayers of God's saints were equivalent, henceforward, to battalions of soldiers.

What the telescope is to the eye, the bicycle to the foot, the telephone to the voice, and the electricity-driven machine to the hand, in enlarging and increasing human power, that is prayer to the soul, because it links us with the mighty power of God, it touches springs that unloose spiritual forces which are eternal in their duration and universal in their scope. "Mighty is he who is mighty in prayer; he has learned how to labor with the energies of God." Why, O soul of man, wilt thou not lay thy fingers on the keyboard of the eternal powers, which would respond instantly to the touch! How great a mistake and loss it is for thee to be satisfied with the lower keyboards of the natural and intellect, when the spiritual, the highest and furthest-reaching, awaits thee!

Samuel viewed prayer as a divine instinct. For him to thwart the promptings towards prayer which arose within his soul would be nothing short of sin. "God forbid," he said, "that I should sin against Him in ceasing to pray."

Let us recognize, we may say with another, that, logic or no logic, men pray, and they want to pray. The instinct to do so seems to be part of ourselves. Probably it is not constant, and it is only the saint who remains in the spirit of prayer; but some time or other, and always when the spiritual nature stirs within us, we begin to pray. Prayer is therefore more than petition, it is the movement of the spirit Godward. We recognize our own limitations and attempt to reach beyond them into the infinite. Therefore, in every true prayer there is much that cannot be put in words. "The Spirit maketh intercession with groanings that cannot be uttered."

To thwart this instinct, whether it prompts us to pray for ourselves or for others, is to do violence to our noblest nature, to grieve the Holy Spirit of God, and to sin against the divine order. Prayerlessness is not only an indication of a besotted and demoralized nature, but is in itself a sin that requires confession and cleansing in the blood of the Cross. And when, in answer to our lowly supplications, we are again brought nigh by the blood of Christ, we shall find that prayer will rise as naturally and freely in our hearts as a fountain from unseen depths fed from the everlasting hills. Prayer is the response of the soul to God, the return tide from us to Him, the sending back in vapor what we receive in showers of heavenly rain.

Samuel viewed prayer as a trusteeship. He could no longer act as judge, but he felt that the interests of the nation had been entrusted to his hands for the highest ends, and it would be treachery to fail in conserving and extending them at least by his intercessions. Often must he have gone aside, as Moses on the Mount, and as our Lord on the hills that engirdled the blue waters of Galilee, to pour out his soul in strong cryings and tears for his brethren, his kinsmen according to the flesh, who were Israelites, to whom pertained the adoption, and the glory, and the covenants, and the giving of the law, and the service of God, and the promises. Often, like the Apostle Paul, he had great heaviness and continual sorrow in his heart. Often, when the Philistines overran the land and oppressed the people with their tyranny, it must have seemed as though his heart would break. The failure of Saul to realize his ideal only elicited the more strenuous appeals to God to save both king and people, and the victory which we must record in our next chapter must have been due to his eager entreaties.

This is a model which we may all copy. The one question for the Church in the present day is whether she may reckon on a new manifestation of the power of the Holy Spirit, and this is entirely contingent on another question: "Is it possible to bring the whole Church to her knees?" If these words are of weight with any, let me ask them to join in one persevering and heaven-moving appeal to God that He would awake, as in the ancient days, in the generations of old, and do great things like those of which our fathers have told us.

15

THE CAUSES OF SAUL'S DOWNFALL

(1 Samuel 13:13–14)

"Bide thou thy time!
Watch with meek eyes the race of pride and crime,
Sit in the gate, and be the heathen's jest,
Smiling and self-possest,
O thou, to whom is pledged a victor's sway,
Bide thou the victor's day."

N. H. J.

THIS chapter is the story of a great tragedy, since it contains the history of the incident which revealed Saul's unfitness to be the founder of a line of kings. Had he stood this test, there is no doubt that he would have been not only the first monarch of Israel but the father of a royal race, and the whole after-history of the chosen people might have been different. But, as we shall see— though at first his kingdom augured prosperity to his fatherland— it evidently lacked the elements of permanence and continuity and of becoming Israel's permanent bulwark against the invasions of the enemy from without and the cancer of disintegration or corruption within.

Let us gather around this story, not only because it has so much to do with the history of God's people but because it is full of instruction for ourselves. Turning from Saul to David, Samuel said, "The Lord hath sought Him a man after His own heart." It is clear, therefore, that in some way Saul had ceased to be "a man after God's own heart," and it becomes us carefully to inquire the reason, that we may avoid the rocks on which this good ship split and foundered.

You will notice that the chapter which tells the history of this tragedy, the overcasting of a bright morning, the spoiling of a fair and beautiful promise, also contains the story of the unutterable distress to which the chosen people had been reduced by another invasion of the Philistines. We are told, for instance, in verse 6, that the people of Israel were in a strait, that they were distressed, that they hid themselves in caves and thickets, in rocks and in pits; indeed, some of them even crossed the Jordan and forsook their fatherland in the hour of its extremity; while those who were yet associated with Saul and Jonathan, as the nucleus of the royal army, followed him trembling (v. 7). A spirit of fearfulness had settled down upon the whole people; the old national spirit had decayed; it seemed as though they could never again be induced to stand against the Philistines, any more than a flock of sheep against a pack of wolves.

We are also informed of the numbers of the vast host of Philistines which had been gathered from all parts in order to crush out the movement towards a national existence, of which the coronation of Saul and the exploits of Jonathan were symptoms (v. 3). We can overhear the tidings brought to Saul (v. 5) by some panic-stricken messenger, who, with the exaggeration of abject fear, described the Philistines as the sand which is on the seashore in multitude.

A further proof of the hapless misery of the people is adduced in verse 19: there was no smith found throughout the whole land of Israel, and the Hebrews had to take their implements of agriculture down to the smithies of the Philistines in order that they might be sharpened for their use. Never in the history of the chosen people was there more dire calamity, more absolute hopelessness and despair, than reigned around Saul and throughout the entire country at this hour.

At this juncture Saul seems to have withdrawn his troops, such as they were, from Michmash and to have taken up his position on the ancient site of Gilgal, where the act of circumcision was performed after Israel had crossed the Jordan under Joshua. There upon the level land, and therefore exposed to the assault of the Philistine hosts at any moment, Saul seems to have pitched his camps, while his heroic son, Jonathan, kept up a post of observation in the vicinity of the Philistine hosts.

While Saul with his soldiers remained at Gilgal, every day marked the diminution of his host. This man and that stole away, either across the Jordan as a fugitive or to hide in some hole and corner of the hills.

It may be asked why, at such a time, Saul did not make one desperate effort against the Philistines. Why did he wait there day after day while his army evaporated before his eyes? Ah! thereby hangs a story—to understand which we must turn back a page or two in the inspired record. In 1 Samuel 10:8, in that early morning interview, when Samuel designated Saul for the crown, he told him that the crisis of his life would overtake him at Gilgal, a prophecy the fulfillment of which had now arrived. "Thou shalt go down before me to Gilgal; and, behold, I will come down unto thee, to offer burnt offerings, and to sacrifice sacrifices of peace offerings; seven days shalt thou tarry, till I come unto thee, and show thee what thou shalt do."

I. SAUL'S MISTAKE.—This command, uttered three years before to Saul, as he stood on the threshold of his vast opportunities, involved two things, and each of them constituted a supreme test.

First, whether he was prepared to act as God's vicegerent, not as absolute monarch determining his own policy and acting on his own initiative, but as God's servant, receiving the marching orders of his life through the prophet's lips; not acting as an autocrat, but as one to whom there had been a delegation of divine authority.

Second, whether he could control his impetuous nature, put the curb upon his impulse, and hold himself well in hand.

It was this embargo which Samuel had laid upon him that made him wait, day after day. Can you not imagine how his chosen advisers and warriors would come around him and urge him to do something? Might they not have pointed to the Philistine hosts encamped at Michmash, gathering like a cloud of storm? Might they not have told him how, unless he acted quickly, his paternal estate would be wiped out before the invasion? Might they not have pointed to the dwindling hosts and said, "Rise up and do something. It would be better to die beneath the Philistines' hand than allow them to pounce down on you as the bird of prey on the trembling dove!"

But he waited, day after day. "He tarried seven days, according to the set time that Samuel had appointed; but Samuel came not to Gilgal, and the people were scattered from him." Then it would seem that within a brief space of the expiry of the allotted time he could wait no more. He thought that Samuel must have forgotten the appointment, or had been intercepted in making his way from Ramah through the Philistine lines. He had waited till within half an hour (because to offer a burnt offering and a peace offering could not take much longer), and then spoiled the whole by his inability to delay further; and he said to the priest, who still lingered by the ancient site where God had been worshiped and the tabernacle posted, "Bring hither the ephod, and let us offer the sacrifice." "And it came to pass that as soon as he had made an end of offering the burnt offering, behold, Samuel came."

Ah, if only some sentry standing on a pinnacle of rock could have looked over into the adjacent valley and seen the form of the old man drawing nearer to the camp he might have warned the king, crying, "Samuel is coming." But there was no one to arrest him, nothing but the monition and remonstrance of his own heart. It was shown that he could not wait for God in absolute faith that He could not fail nor deceive. He was careful to maintain an outward rite, but the spirit of devotion and faith was altogether wanting. As he was, his successors would become, to the undoing of Israel; therefore his kingdom could not continue.

The one lesson that comes back to us with almost overwhelming force is that the man who is after God's heart is the man who will obey God to the letter, who will wait for God to the last moment, who will dare to stand amid a diminishing and dwindling army, and even see disaster imminent, but, because he has not received the marching orders of God, will stand still, until presently God sets him free.

How many religious people there are, who, as they review their past life, can recall moments when they did not know what to do. An inner voice—still, sweet, but commanding—bade them wait and trust; but many other voices, loud and strident, summoned them to act; so that the still small voice of faith, of resignation, of absolute obedience was silenced, the one rash word spoken, the one irrevocable act performed, betraying the weakness of the heart, the ineffectiveness of the resolve. When all was over, Samuel has come, and we have reproached ourselves, saying, "Oh, if I had only thought that God was so near, I would not have acted as I did. Woe is me; why could not I wait?" Samuel always comes just at the last moment, but it is so hard to wait till he does come. "'Master, Master, we perish'; and He arose, and rebuked the storm, and said, 'Why are ye fearful, O ye of little faith?'" God hath not given us the spirit of fear, but the spirit of power, of love, and of self-discipline and self-restraint.

Man becomes so weary of waiting, and it seems as though God is so slow. God's mighty processes sweep around a wide orbit. One day is as a thousand years, but He is coming as the morning, as the spring, as the millennium. "His going forth is sure as the morning, and He shall come unto us as the rain, as the latter rain that watereth the earth."

II. SAUL'S DISINGENUOUS PLEA.—Notice Saul's explanation to Samuel. He said: "I said to myself, 'The Philistines will come down upon me to Gilgal, and I have not entreated the favor of the Lord.' I forced myself therefore, and offered the burnt offering." That surely was insincere. He laid the blame on circumstances; he said practically: "The circumstances of my lot forced my hand; I did not want to do it, I was most reluctant, but felt compelled—the Philistines were coming. I tell you the scepter was wrested from my grasp, and I had to obey the imperious voice of the misfortunes that fell thick and fast upon me." His speech reminds us of Aaron's, who stripped the people naked before God and their enemies and sought to excuse himself by saying, "They gave me their earrings; I cast them into the fire, and there came out this calf."

We are all prone to speak in the same tone. When the rash word has been uttered and the proud act done; when we have refused to obey, and have seen the house of our life toppling down upon us, or consuming in the flames of our folly, then we have said, "Circumstances compelled me—I had to do it, and I did it; I forced myself—my hand was forced."

O soul of man, thou art greater than circumstances; greater than things; greater than the mob of evil counselors. Thou art meant to be God's crowned and enthroned king; to rule and not to be ruled; to obey God only, and to resist all other attempts to bring thee under the yoke. Rouse thee, lest it should be said of thee also, that thy kingdom shall not continue.

III. MARK THE ALTERNATE TO THIS.—In answer to all this, Samuel, speaking in the name of God, said, "I have chosen a man after My own heart, who shall perform all My will." In Jesse's home the lad was being prepared who could believe and not make haste. Listen to the manner in which this man after God's own heart spoke in after-years: "I waited patiently for the Lord, and He inclined unto me, and heard my cry. He brought me up also out of an horrible pit, out of the miry clay, and He set my feet upon a rock and established my goings. And He hath put a new song in my mouth, even praise unto our God; many shall see it, and fear, and shall trust in the Lord. Blessed is the man that maketh the Lord his trust, and respecteth not the proud, nor such as turn aside to lies" (Ps. 40:1–4).

Wait, wait thou thy Lord's leisure. Let your heart stop its feverish beating, and your pulse register no more its tumultuous waves of emotion! To act now would only disappoint the highest hopes, mar the divine purposes, and set stones rolling that shall never be stopped. Wait for God, stand still and see His salvation. His servant is coming up the pass; his steps may not be quite so speedy as we would have them, but he will arrive to the moment; not a moment too soon, but not a moment too late. God's messenger is timed to come when the heart has almost failed, the steps almost gone, and hope almost vanished. "The Lord is at hand!" Oh, wait, my soul! Wait, wait upon God, for God cannot be behind, as He will not be before, the allotted and appointed moment.

And when He comes there will be laughter for tears, harvest for sowing, blue skies for clouds, and long days of rapturous bliss that shall make thee forget the shame and reproach of the past!

16

"TWO PUTTING TEN THOUSAND
TO FLIGHT"

(1 Samuel 14)

"Oh! I have seen the day,
When with a single word—
God helping me to say
'My trust is in the Lord!'
My soul hath quelled a thousand foes,
Fearless of all that could oppose."

COWPER

JUST two young men, with the glow of patriotism in their hearts, and trust in God as their guiding star—what may they not effect?

Jonathan was a true knight of God, who anticipated some of the noblest traits of Christian chivalry. We may almost say of him that he was the Hebrew Bayard, a soldier without fear and without reproach. He lived pure, spoke true, righted wrong, was faithful to the high claims of human love, and followed the Christ, though as yet he knew Him not. His character serves as a bright background on which that of his father is but a sorry contrast.

From the Jordan bank a noble valley, twelve miles in length, leads up into the hill country of central Palestine, and so to the seaboard of the Mediterranean. Two miles from the head of this defile, and about eight miles due north of Jerusalem, the cliffs on either side become very precipitous and approach each other almost to touching.

Conceive of a very narrow pass protected on either side by steep walls of chalky formation on which only the wild goats could find a footing, and almost unscalable by man. The ridge on the north, which rises above an almost perpendicular crag into three knolls, was called Bozez, or "shining," because it reflects all day the full light of the Eastern sun, while that on the south, a few yards distant, was known as Seneh, "the acacia," being constantly in the shade. Michmash crowned the former, and there the Philistines were encamped, while the little village of Geba lay above the latter, and thither Saul had removed his army, such as it was, withdrawing from Gilgal in the plains of the Jordan to watch the movements of the hostile force.

How long the armies watched each other we have no means of knowing, nor can we guess what the result might have been had it not been for the heroic episode which we are to recount; but it is certain that Israel was absolutely spiritless. At the most the men of war who gathered around the pomegranate tree where Saul had pitched his tent numbered only 600, and these had only such rude weapons as clubs and goads.

Jonathan chafed at the inaction and the disgrace which the whole situation attached to his countrymen. He was animated also by a profound faith in God, and was prompted by the Divine Spirit to an act which issued in a glorious victory and deliverance.

I. JONATHAN ENTERED INTO THE DIVINE PURPOSE.—It seemed to him impossible to suppose that God had forsaken the people of His choice or withdrawn from His ancient covenant. Had He promised, and could He not perform? Were not the people of Israel His chosen heritage? Had He not chosen them out of all the world that they might be the custodians and purveyors of divine truth to the nations? Was not the land of Canaan made over to them by an irrevocable deed of gift? Did not all the miraculous leadings and interpositions of the past confirm such an interpretation of the divine purpose? Surely, then, the present state of things could not be according to the divine will! Surely the purpose of the Almighty was in conflict with the invasion of the land by these Philistine hordes, and only waited for some believing soul to enter into full communion with its mighty current and deliverance would be secured!

Saul, on the other hand, had no perception of these things. The great past failed to speak to him. Discouraged by what met his eye and ear from morning to night, he had no power to rouse himself to lay hold on the divine promise of deliverance. The sentence of deposition, which Samuel had so recently pronounced, like a stone on the mouth of a tomb, seemed to shut him up to despair.

It is of the utmost importance in this mortal life, when heart and flesh fail before the giant wrongs that assert themselves against the well-being of mankind—such as the drink traffic, the mania for betting and gambling, impurity, and the insensate absorption in pleasure, which are the Philistines of our time—to look away to the divine purpose as disclosed in the redemption achieved on the cross by the blood of the world's Redeemer. Surely that cannot have been shed in vain. The power and potency of the divine might are pledged to realize and accomplish that full deliverance of which the cross was prophecy. The Son of Man has been manifested that He might destroy the works of the devil; and He will not fail nor be discouraged until that purpose has been realized. Happy are they who, like Jonathan, raise themselves above the depression of the moment in living fellowship with these eternal facts, and ally their weakness and helplessness with the march of God as He is ever going forth to establish righteousness and judgment in the earth, which has been redeemed by precious blood.

II. He Yielded Himself as an Instrument.—God always works through human means. He calls us into fellowship with Himself, so that the divine tides shall flow through human channels. He will multiply the bread, but He requires human hands to distribute it. He raises the dead, but man must roll away the stone and unwrap the cerements of the grave. He arrests Saul of Tarsus, but the words and patience of suffering saints must be the goad which surely urges the disloyal soul to repent. God is ever on the outlook for believing souls who will receive His power and grace on the one hand and transmit them on the other. He chooses them that by them He should make His mighty power known. Happy are they who are not insensible to the divine impulse, nor disobedient to the heavenly vision.

Jonathan was one of those blessed souls who are as sensitive to God as the retina of the eye to light, or the healthy muscle to the nerve; and "it fell upon a day that he said unto the young man that bore his armor, 'Come, let us go over to the Philistines' garrison, that is on the other side.'" With a beautiful modesty "he told not his father"; and in all probability the two slipped away silently in the gray dawn, while their comrades were still wrapped in slumber. The intimation of a divine purpose thrilled the ardent spirit of the young prince, to which he gave some clue in the words "It may be that the Lord will work for us, for there is no restraint to the Lord to save by many or by few."

Notice where Jonathan laid the emphasis. He had the smallest possible faith in himself and the greatest faith in God. His soul waited for the Lord; in Him was centered all his hope, and from His gracious help he expected great things. All that he aspired to was to be the humble vehicle through which the delivering grace of God might work. This is what God wants—not our strength, but our weakness which in absolute despair turns to Him; not our armies, but two or three elect souls who expect great things and dare them. It is false to say that the Almighty is on the side of great battalions. All history goes to show that the movements which have transformed the face of the world have been achieved by the going forth of God through individuals—men and women who have not been specially distinguished by outstanding talents but have been led to surrender themselves absolutely to the divine impulse. What shall I more say?—for time would fail to tell of Carey, and Wilberforce, and Livingstone, and George Müller, and hundreds more.

Yield yourselves to God—and I especially appeal to the young men who may read these words. There are wrongs that God wants to right, tyrannies He is about to break, foes of human peace and happiness that He wants to quell; but He must have agents and instruments, clean and pure, true and faithful, delivered from the domination of the flesh and absolutely resigned to His disposal. It matters not if they be highborn, as Jonathan, or as obscure as his armorbearer; through them He will achieve a great deliverance.

Saul, the chosen king, had no such vision and no such faith. He was not able to hear the divine voice speaking in his soul, but had to depend on the interposition of the priest (v. 19 and 36). He spoke and acted as though the victory depended wholly on the efforts that he and his men might put forth, and by his oath forbidding the eating of any food until evening he forfeited the full results of God's interposition. Could it be supposed that God's deliverance of His people would fall short because they put forth the ends of the rods that might be in their hands to convey a bit of wild honey to their lips? Throughout the whole day, and especially in his senseless adjuration which was meant to save time but really hindered the full result, Saul showed himself oblivious of the one thought that animated the heart of his noble son—that God was working through human instruments to inflict His own judgment on the invading hosts.

III. JONATHAN RECKONED ON GOD, AND GOD DID NOT FAIL HIM.—Faith is the indomitable power by which we call unto our help a whole range of laws and forces which are outside the lives of ordinary men. As we have said, they have two keyboards to their organ, we have three. They employ the physical and intellectual, while we, in addition, may call in the aid of the spiritual and eternal. Thus we are able to accomplish the same results, and better, by the assistance of energies which are as much greater than those ordinarily employed as electricity is greater than horse-power, or steam than hand. This was the secret of Jonathan's success.

As they ascended the steep cliff-side, the young men agreed on the sign which should indicate that they were indeed in the line of the divine will and that God would not fail them. The heart of man, in its first venture on the way of faith, eagerly longs for some sign that it is not following a will-o'-the-wisp or being misled by wreckers' lights. This was graciously granted in the mocking voices of the advanced outposts which ridiculed the idea that the Hebrews were to be feared (14:11–12) even though they should succeed in scaling the crags. "Behold," they said, "the Hebrews come forth out of the holes where they have hid themselves." Then the men of the garrison shouted to Jonathan and his armorbearer, "Come up to us, and we will show you a thing [or, we should like to make your acquaintance]!"

This was the heaven-given sign and conveyed the assurance that the Lord had already delivered them into the hand of Israel (v. 10). By faith the soul appropriates the divine answer. "Whatsoever we ask, we receive of Him." But it is only as we fulfill the one all-important condition of successful prayer, which is so often overlooked: "All things whatsoever ye pray and ask for, *believe that ye have received them,* and ye shall have them" (Mark 11:24).

The soul that reckons on God cannot be ashamed. When they reached the top, the two young Benjamites used their slings with such precision that twenty men measured their length on the ground, and a trembling from God, a heaven-sent panic, spread from them back on the main army behind and to the bands of spoilers returning from their night raids. The Philistines could not know that the two who faced them were absolutely alone. It seemed as though they were precursors of a host of resolute and desperate men, and, suddenly, in the panic, each man suspected his neighbor of being in league against him. The foreign mercenaries and strangers, of whom there was a large admixture, became the objects of special terror; "and every man's sword was against his fellow, so that there was a very great discomfiture." Meanwhile the Hebrews who had been allied to the Philistines or silently acquiescent to their rule, even they also turned against them; and all who had hid themselves in the hill country of Ephraim, when they heard that the Philistines fled, even they also followed hard after them in battle.

From his outlook at Geba, Saul beheld the wild confusion, and how the multitude swayed to and fro and melted away. Without delay, he hurled himself with his soldiers on the flying foe, who fled, in headlong precipitancy, down the long valley, past Beth-aven, past the Upper and then the Lower Beth-horon, in order to gain the Philistine frontier by the valley of Aijalon. Every town through which the fugitives passed rose in their rear and joined the pursuit, so that the flying host was greatly reduced, and thousands of warriors dyed the highways of the land, which they had so grievously oppressed, with their heart's blood. Thus did God work on behalf of His chosen people in answer to Jonathan's faith.

The unwise prohibition of the king against food had a terrible sequel, first, in the exhaustion of the troops and, secondly, in the famished eating of the spoils of the day without the proper separation of the blood. Still worse, when the day closed in and Saul asked counsel of God, the divine oracle was unresponsive. Some sin had silenced it, and the monarch, already touched with the dark suspicions and fears in which his soul became afterward so densely enveloped, realized that some sin was crying for discovery and expiation. He did not look for that sin where he would have assuredly found it, in his own heart, but in the people that stood around him. Finally, he and Jonathan stood before the people as the objects of the divine displeasure, and Saul was prepared even to sacrifice his son in his moody wrath.

But the people saved him. They cried indignantly, "Shall Jonathan die, who hath wrought this great salvation in Israel? God forbid! As the Lord liveth, there shall not one hair of his head fall to the ground, for he hath wrought with God this day." Ah, the cause of discomfiture most surely lay between those two men; but it was not due to anything in Jonathan. Saul alone was to blame. He had not only missed the greatest opportunity of his life, but he was already enwrapping himself in the unbelief, the jealousy and moroseness of temper in which his sun was to be enshrouded while it was yet day.

17

FAILURE UNDER THE SUPREME TEST

(1 Samuel 15:26)

"Mortal, if life smile on thee, and thou find
All to thy mind,
Think, who did once from Heaven to Hell descend
Thee to befriend!
So shalt thou dare forego at His dear call
Thy Best—thine All."

KEBLE

ON the shores of the Dead Sea, encrusted with salt, lie the trunks of many noble trees which have been torn from their roots and carried by the rapid Jordan in its flow from the uplands of Galilee toward the depression of that remarkable gorge; and as they line those desolate shores they remind us of lives which God planted to bear fruit and give shade which have not fulfilled His original purpose in their creation, and which have been torn up by the roots and borne down to the sea of death. Conspicuous among such failures is that of Saul, the first king of Israel.

It is impossible to turn to these pages without lamenting that the bright promise of his early life was so soon overcast; and that he, who stood forth in the morning of his life amid the acclaim of his people as likely to do marvelous work for his fatherland, became one of those whom the sacred writers describe as having failed of the high purpose of their life, been rejected in their mission, and cast away as tools from the hands of the great Artificer.

This chapter gives the story of the final rejection of Saul, which had indeed been threatened aforetime but which now befell.

I. THE TEST OF THE DIVINE SUMMONS AND COMMAND.—"Go and smite Amalek, and utterly destroy all that they have, and spare them not; but slay both man and woman, infant and suckling, ox and sheep, camel and ass" (v. 3).

This command was given after several years had intervened from the incident narrated in the previous chapter; and during those years Saul had met with marvelous encouragement. The handful of men who had followed him, trembling, had increased to a great army, properly disciplined and armed, and led by Abner, his uncle. He had also waged very successful wars against Moab and the children of Ammon on the east, against Edom on the south, and against the kings of Zobah on the north. In whatever direction he had directed his arms, he had been victorious beyond his highest hopes. It is also evident that he had gathered around him considerable grandeur, for we find the royal table was reserved for himself, Abner and Jonathan; that he was surrounded by a bodyguard of runners; and that his will was law. The kingdom that had been inaugurated amid such adverse circumstances was beginning to enforce respect, and Saul was able to vie, both in the magnificence of his state and in the army that followed him, with the kings of the lands that bordered on Canaan.

It was at this time that the supreme test entered his life, as it so often comes to us in days of prosperity. In the warm summer days we are most in dread of corruption and contagion, and it is in the days of prosperity that the soul is oftenest subjected, not realizing the significance of the ordeal, to its supreme test. If of late you have had immunity from special adversity, if your circumstances have been easy and comfortable, if paths that were once difficult have become smooth and easy—be on your guard; for, at such a time as ye think not, the Son of Man comes to call you to His bar.

You will notice, also, that this supreme test gave him a final chance of retrieving the past. At Gilgal, years before, God had told him by the lips of Samuel that his kingdom would not continue; but there had been no sentence of his deposition or rejection, and so it seems as though this last command was put into his life to give him an opportunity of wiping out his former failure and mistake—of retrieving the fortunes that had seemed to be absolutely sacrificed.

God often comes to us when we have made some sad and apparently irretrievable mistake. He gives us yet another opportunity of reversing the past, as when our Lord said to His disciples in the Garden of the Olive Press: "Sleep on now, and take your rest"; a moment afterward adding, "Arise, let us be going," as though a fresh opportunity would be afforded of fellowship in His sufferings.

The divine command involved the absolute extermination of the Amalekites; for the word translated "utterly destroy" would be better rendered *devote*. It is the word so often used in the book of Joshua for placing under the ban the sin-infected cities of the Canaanites. It was understood that, in the case of the "devoted" city, man, woman and child, and the very beasts, must be destroyed; even its precious metals could be kept only after being passed through the fires of purification (Num. 31:21ff.). With such absolute devastation and destruction was the name of Amalek to be wiped out from under heaven.

There had been feuding between Amalek and Israel from the earliest days. "Thus saith the Lord of hosts, 'I have marked that which Amalek did to Israel, how he set himself against him in the way, when he came up out of Egypt'" (v. 2). You will remember that Moses reared an altar and called it Jehovah-nissi—"the Lord my banner"—because he said that the Lord would have war with

Amalek until He had wiped out the reproach of His people (Ex. 17:16). Centuries had passed, and this ancient threat had remained unfulfilled until this hour, and now the command was given, "Go and smite Amalek."

At first it seems very terrible that God demanded this act of obedience from Saul; but on the other hand the Amalekites, as we are told in verse 18, were sinners of a very black and aggravated type. "Utterly destroy the sinners, the Amalekites, and fight against them until they be consumed." We learn also from verse 33 that Agag with his sword had often made women childless. A very cruel and rapacious tribe of robbers were these Amalekites, who were constantly making raids upon the southern frontier of Judah. It was absolutely necessary, therefore, for the safety of the chosen people, that their power to injure should be permanently arrested and their claws drawn.

Even in this world God sets up His judgment seat; and as our Saviour tells us in His last wonderful discourse, the Son of Man sits upon the throne of His glory, while the nations are gathered before Him, and He separates them as the sheep from the goats. These words, without doubt, portend some imposing event, which we are to witness in that great day when the King of the Ages will call to His bar every nation and kindred, people and tongue, and will announce His awards. But we cannot suppose, for a single moment, that the judgment of the nations is to be altogether relegated to that final day. Throughout the history of the world the nations have been standing before Christ's bar. Nineveh stood there, Babylon stood there, Greece and Rome stood there, Spain and France stood there, and Great Britain is standing there today. One after another has had the solemn award—*depart*, and they have passed into a destruction which has been absolute and irretrievable.

The Amalekites had stood before the bar of God, had been weighed in His balances and found wanting. Their sentence had been pronounced, and Saul was called upon to inflict it. But remember that Saul was only doing summarily and suddenly that which otherwise would follow in the natural process of decay, for God has so constituted us that when we sin against the laws of truth, purity and righteousness, decay immediately sets in by an inevitable law. If Amalek had never been attacked by Saul and his hosts, the vices that were already at work in the heart of the people must have led to the utter undoing and consumption of the nation. It is said of families in our great cities, infected with the evils that are rife among us, that in five generations they die out, having lost the power of self-propagation; and what is true of a family is equally so of a nation. We may infer that there was therefore mercy in this divine ordinance. It was infinitely better for Amalek, and for the surrounding peoples which would have become infected by her slow deterioration, that by one stroke of the executioner's axe the existence of the nation should be brought to an end.

II. OBEDIENCE WITH RESERVE.—The story is told us in verse 9: "But Saul and the people spared Agag." When he raised his standard, 200,000 footmen from Israel and 10,000 men of Judah, Benjamin and Simeon gathered around it at Telaim, on the southern frontier; and they came to the chief city of Amalek, which lay, probably, a little to the south of Beer-sheba.

After lying in ambush in some dry watercourse, or wady, and having given notice to the Kenites—a peaceful, friendly people—to depart, the attacking army carried the city by assault, put to the sword men, women and children, and pursued the fleeing remnants of the Amalekites from Havilah even to Shur, at the boundary of Egypt. With the exception of Agag and a few who may have escaped, and the best of the flocks and herds, the whole country was rid of its inhabitants and reduced to the deathlike silence of an awful solitude.

Saul returned, flushed with triumph, reared a monument of

victory in the oasis of Carmel, near to Hebron; and then came down to the sacred site of Gilgal, that he might sacrifice to the Lord, and perhaps divide the vast plunder of sheep and goats, of oxen and camels, which had fallen into his hands and which he and the people had been loath to destroy. "Saul and the people spared Agag, and the best of the sheep and of the oxen, and of the fatlings, and the lambs, and all that was good, and would not utterly destroy them; but everything that was vile and refuse, they destroyed utterly."

Whether this reserve was due, so far as Saul was concerned, to greed, as appears most likely, or because, as he says in verse 24, he feared to thwart the people, obeying their voice rather than the voice of God, we cannot decide; but considerable light is thrown on the incident by the startling expression used by Samuel in verse 19, when he says, "Why didst thou fly upon the spoil?" employing the same expression as in chapter 14:32, where we are told that the people, in their ravenous hunger, flew upon the spoil and ate even with the blood. The same passionate vehemence seems to have characterized Saul and the men of Israel. Surely rapacity and greed were at work, and before their boiling currents all the bulwarks of principle and conscience were swept away.

There is great significance in this for us all. We are prepared to obey the divine commands up to a certain point, and there we stop. Just as soon as "the best and choicest" begin to be touched, we draw the line and refuse further compliance. We listen to soft voices that bid us stay our hand when our Isaac is on the altar. We are quite prepared to give up that which costs us nothing—our money, but not our children—to the missionary cause; the things which are clearly and disgracefully wrong, but not the self-indulgences which are peculiarly fascinating to our temperament. Skin for skin, yea, all that a man hath, will he give for his life—only spare him that, and he will cheerfully renounce his claim to all else. There is always a tendency with the best of us to make a bargain with God and sacrifice all to His will, if only He will permit us to spare Agag and the best of the spoil.

But an even deeper reading of this story is permissible. Throughout the Bible Amalek stands for the flesh, having sprung from the stock of Esau, who, for a morsel of meat, steaming fragrantly in the air, sold his birthright. To spare the best of Amalek is surely equivalent to sparing some root of evil, some plausible indulgence, some favorite sin. For us, Agag must stand for that evil propensity, which exists in all of us, for self-gratification; and to spare Agag is to be merciful to ourselves, to exonerate and palliate our failures, and to condone our besetting sin.

Is this your case? You are willing to give Christ the key of every cupboard in your heart, save one; but that contains your most cherished sin, for which you find manifold excuses, and to retain which you are prepared to sacrifice everything else. Thus Ananias and Sapphira kept back part of the price and were cut off from the ranks of the Church.

It is startling to learn that Saul perished, on the field of Gilboa, by the hand of an Amalekite (2 Sam. 1:1–10). What a remarkable fact! The least instructed can decipher the lesson. He who runs may read. If we spare ourselves, forbearing to cut off the right hand or foot which may be causing us to offend, we shall certainly perish by the hand of that which we refused to part with. Our cherished indulgences will bring about our undoing. The love of God, foreseeing the risk we are incurring, pleads with us to destroy without mercy the enemies of our own peace; but Agag comes to us delicately, we forbear to inflict the divine sentence, and presently we are stricken down by the hand of the assassin, dye the greensward with our lifeblood, and are despoiled of our crown, which is transferred to another.

Moreover, presently, Samuel arrives to speak the divine sentence of deposition: "Because thou hast rejected the word of the Lord, the Lord hath rejected thee from being king."

18

A REMARKABLE COLLOQUY

(1 Samuel 15:12–35)

"Thy choice was earth! Thou didst attest
'Twas fitter spirit should subserve
The flesh, than flesh refuse to nerve
Beneath the spirit's play! Thou art shut
Out of the heaven of spirit! Glut
Thy sense upon the world! 'tis thine
Forever!—take it!"

R. B.

AN INTIMATION of Saul's lapsed obedience was made in the secret ear of Samuel in the dead of night, when God came near to him and said, "It repenteth Me that I have set up Saul to be king, for he hath turned back from following Me, and hath not performed My commandments."

God requires literal obedience, and when that fails the results are as though He had changed His purpose or repented, but this is in appearance only. As a matter of fact, God cannot repent or change His purpose. Man may frustrate the working out of His plan, but the Almighty Workman will achieve it by some other method.

The wind may be blowing steadily in the same direction, and as long as we yield to it, it will waft us to the desired haven; but it is always possible for us to reverse our course and go against it, and then our life is so powerfully affected that it would seem as though God had changed His purpose—the change being due to ourselves, because, whereas formerly we moved with His purpose, now by disobedience or unbelief we are steadily resisting it.

Does God ever come to you at night, or when the world is quiet, and tell you His secrets? Happy are they whom God can trust with His own profound sorrow over the failure of His chosen servants, honoring them with His confidence and appealing to them to watch with Him. "Shall I hide from Abraham that which I do?"

The faithful soul of Samuel was deeply moved. We are told he was "*angry*"(R. V.)—a righteous indignation that one who had been appointed with such solemn sanctions, and had bidden fair to achieve such glorious deliverances for his people, had so seriously missed his mark. Those who are true to God cannot but feel indignant when His purposes are frustrated and His grace outraged, and the door of usefulness which He had set wide in front of a chosen servant is shut and barred by some act of careless or willful disobedience. Samuel's soul was not only deeply moved but "he cried unto the Lord all night." Ah! how much we owe to the Divine Friend, and to human friends who, when they see deterioration at work in us, take no rest and give God no rest. This is the most priceless service that one soul can afford another. There is hope so long as lover and friend bear up our case before God and plead that rather they should be accursed than that we should perish. How many a son now leading a reckless and profligate life, in his still hours, or when his evil courses have cast him on a bed of sickness and debarred him from the active pursuits of life, comforts himself with the thought that, in some lone cottage, his mother does not cease to pray for him, and he secretly hopes that her prayers may avail against the vehemence of the fiery passions by which his soul is driven.

Samuel traveled some fifteen miles to find Saul, following him from Carmel where, as we have seen, he seems to have set up a monument which was either shaped in the form of a hand or on which the figure of a hand was graved (R.V. margin), to Gilgal, the site of the ancient shrine where, as one of the versions informs us, the king was engaged in offering sacrifices to Jehovah, and there this most remarkable colloquy took place.

SAUL.—It was commenced by the king who, seeing the prophet coming towards him, advanced to meet him with an unctuous phrase upon his lips, "Blessed be thou of the Lord," and, with great complacency in his demeanor, added, "I have performed the commandment of the Lord." Whether Saul was blinded and did not really know how far he had deteriorated, for it is certain that disobedience puts out our eyes, as Hubert did young Arthur's, blinding us to the enormity of our sin, or whether he desired to gloss over his failure and to appear as a truly obedient son, so as to deceive the prophet, we cannot tell, but that "Blessed be thou of the Lord," from *his* lips, and at *such* a moment, has an ugly sound. It reminds one of certain persons who interlard their business talk with references to religion, so that they may put the unwary off their guard and enable their user to take a mean advantage, under the appearance of a high code of morals. It is the sin of Judas who betrayed his Master with a kiss. Better the open foe than the secret assassin. Better a dozen times the arrow that flieth by day than the pestilence that walketh in darkness.

SAMUEL.—At that moment the sheep began to bleat and the oxen to low. A breath of wind, laden with the unmistakable indication of the near presence of a great multitude of flocks and herds, was wafted to the prophet's ear. It is an unfortunate occurrence when, just as a man is becoming loud in his protestations of goodness, some such untoward incident suddenly takes place, so that the lowing of the oxen and the bleating of the sheep belie his words. I remember once a professor of religion who desired to impress me with his entire sanctification and deliverance from every kind of idol, giving unmistakable evidence, by the taint of tobacco on his breath while he spoke, that he had been smoking a rather rank kind of tobacco. I had not said a single word about smoking. I have never felt it my business to denounce indulgences concerning which God may not convict men universally. It is our business on matters not clearly forbidden, and concerning which Christian people are not agreed, to lay down general principles and to leave our hearers to apply them for themselves. But when this man went out of his way to assert his entire deliverance, I naturally was more on the alert, and in the taint on his breath I detected the presence of the choice oxen and sheep which had been reserved. With sad irony the prophet said, "What meaneth then this bleating of sheep in mine ears, and the lowing of oxen which I hear?"

SAUL.—The king excused himself by laying emphasis on the word *they*—"*They* have brought them from the Amalekites; for *the people* spared the best of the sheep and of the oxen, to sacrifice unto the Lord thy God." Notice the subtle effort to conciliate the prophet by the emphasis laid upon the word *thy*—"thy God; and the rest we have utterly destroyed." It was unroyal and contemptible to lay the blame upon the people, and it was an excuse which could not be allowed.

SAMUEL.—The royal backslider would probably have gone on speaking, but Samuel interrupted him, saying, "Stay, and I will tell thee what the Lord hath said to me this night." Then the faithful old prophet went back to the past. He reminded Saul how insignificant had been his origin, and how he had shrunk from undertaking the great responsibility of the station to which God had summoned him. He reminded him how he had been raised up to the throne, and how the Almighty King of Israel had delegated to him His authority, requiring that he should act as His designated vicegerent. He reminded him also that a distinct charge had been given him, and that the responsibility of determining his line of action had been transferred from himself, as the agent, to the Divine Being who had issued His mandate of destruction. In spite of all, Saul had allowed his greed to hurry him into an act of disobedience. He had pounced upon the spoil as a hungry lion upon his prey and had done evil in the sight of the Lord.

SAUL.—The king reiterated his poor excuse: "Yea, I have obeyed the voice of the Lord, and have gone the way that the Lord sent me, and have brought Agag, the king of Amalek, and have utterly destroyed the Amalekites. But the people took of the spoil, sheep and oxen, the chief of the devoted things, to sacrifice unto the Lord thy God in Gilgal." It was as though he had said, "You have judged me wrongfully. If you would wait for a little while, you would see the issue of my act of apparent disobedience." He may even have cajoled himself into thinking that he meant to sacrifice these spoils now that he had reached Gilgal; or he might have mentally resolved there and then that he would sacrifice them, and so relieve himself of the complicated position into which he found himself drifting.

SAMUEL.—In answer to this last remark, God's messenger uttered one of the greatest sentences in the earlier books of the Bible, a sentence which is the seed-germ of much to the same purpose in the Prophets, which in subsequent centuries was repeated in different forms, and to which our blessed Lord gave His assent—"Hath the Lord as great delight in burnt offerings and sacrifices, as in obeying the voice of the Lord? Behold, to obey is better than sacrifice, and to hearken than the fat of rams." Whatever Saul might be leading him to infer as to his intention to offer the sacrifice, there could be no doubt that up to that moment, at least, he had disobeyed God's positive command; and, in point of fact, the whole attitude of his soul was towards disobedience and rebellion which, in fact, were the assertion of his own will and way against God's.

Then, tearing the veil aside, the old man showed the enormity of the sin which had been committed, by saying: "Rebellion is equally vile as the sin of witchcraft, and stubbornness is as idolatry and the teraphim." The grosser sins were universally reprobated and held up to contempt by good men, but in God's sight there was equivalence between them and the sin of which the king had been guilty. Then, facing the monarch, and looking at him with his searching eyes, the prophet, in the majesty of his authority as God's representative, pronounced the final sentence of deposition, saying, "Because thou hast rejected the word of the Lord, He hath rejected thee from being king."

SAUL.—In a moment the king realized the brink of the precipice on which he stood; and with the cry not of a penitent, but of a fugitive from justice; not hating his sin, but dreading its result; eager at any cost to keep the crown on his brow and the empire in his hand; afraid of the consequences which might ensue if his leading men detected any break or coolness between himself and the prophet—he cringed before Samuel, saying, "I have sinned; for I have transgressed the commandment of Jehovah, and thy words: because I feared the people, and obeyed their voice. Now therefore, I pray thee, pardon my sin, and turn again with me, that I may worship the Lord."

There is a great difference in the accent with which men utter those words, "*I have sinned.*" The prodigal said them with a faltering voice, not because he feared the consequences of sin, but that he saw its heinousness in the expression of his father's face, and the tears that stood in the beloved eyes. Saul, however, feared the consequences rather than the sin, and that he might avert the sentence he said, as though Samuel had the power of the keys to open and unloose, to pardon or to refuse forgiveness, "Pardon my sin."

SAMUEL.—The prophet saw through the subterfuge. He knew that his penitence was not genuine, but that the king was deceiving him with his words, and he turned about to go away. Then Saul, in the extremity of his anguish, in fear that in losing him he might lose at once his best friend and the respect of the nation, seems to have sprung forward and seized the collar of Samuel's cloak, and as he did so with a strong, masterful grasp, as if to restrain and draw back to himself the retreating figure of the prophet, it rent. When Samuel felt and heard the tear, he said, "The Lord hath rent the kingdom of Israel from thee this day, and hath given it to a neighbor of thine, that is better than thou." And then, referring to Saul's effort to turn him back, as though he would reverse the sentence which he had pronounced, he said, "Remember that the Strength of Israel will not lie nor repent; His sentence is irrevocable. The word is gone out of His lips and cannot be called back. There is no opportunity of changing His mind though thou shalt seek it bitterly and with tears."

Even at that moment, had Saul thrown himself at God's feet and asked for pardon, he would have been accepted and forgiven. Even though as a monarch his kingdom might have passed from him, as a man he would have received pardon. But there are moments in our lives, irrevocable moments, when we take steps that cannot be retraced, when we assume positions from which we cannot retreat, when results are settled never to be reversed.

SAUL.—Again the king repeated the sentence, "I have sinned," but his real meaning was disclosed in the following words: "Yet honor me now before the elders of my people, and before Israel, and turn again with me, that I may worship Jehovah thy God." His inner thought was still to stand well with the people, and he was prepared to make any confession of wrongdoing as a price of Samuel's apparent friendship.

Finally, Samuel stayed with him, that the elders might not become disaffected, and that the people generally might have no idea of the deposition of the king, lest the kingdom itself might totter to its fall before his successor was prepared to take his place.

He stayed therefore. The two knelt side by side before God, but what a contrast! *Here* was darkest night; *there,* the brightness of the day. *Here* was the rejected; *there,* the chosen faithful servant. *Here* was one whose course from that moment was to be enwrapped in the dark clouds of moody tyranny and jealousy, until he died upon the field of Gilboa; *there* was one, the unsullied beauty of whose character was to remain untarnished until his removal to that world where he would shine as the sun, in his heavenly Father's kingdom.

Lastly, the old man summoned Agag, the king of the Amalekites, to his presence, and Agag came to him "*cheerfully,*" hoping without doubt that he would be spared; and saying, as he advanced, "Surely the bitterness of death is past—there is no reason for me to fear it." Then Samuel, strengthened with some paroxysm of righteous indignation, seized a sword that lay within his reach and hewed Agag in pieces before the Lord—this being an emblem of the holy zeal that will give no quarter to the flesh. And we are reminded of the words of the apostle, "Make not provision for the flesh, to fulfill the lusts thereof." To Amalek we must give no quarter.

May God help us to read deeply into this tragic story. Whensoever God our Father puts a supreme test into our lives, let us at any cost obey Him. Everything hinges upon absolute obedience. If you cannot obey, you cannot command. If you do not obey, you are not fit to be an instrument in God's hand. If the chisel is not true, the sculptor dare not hold it still in hand. Let us walk circumspectly and wisely, redeeming each opportunity, that God may make the most possible of us, and that, above all, we may not become castaways.

19

"AN EVIL SPIRIT FROM THE LORD"

(1 Samuel 16:13–14)

"Canst thou not minister to a mind diseased;
Pluck from the memory a rooted sorrow?
Raze out the written troubles of the brain,
And with some sweet, oblivious antidote
Cleanse the stuff'd bosom of that perilous stuff
Which weighs upon the heart?"

SHAKESPEARE

ALL great painters and poets whose works are of the first order have availed themselves of the force of contrast—that
there should be a dark background to set forth some beautiful
and radiant object. The Bible excels in its use of this striking
method of laying emphasis. In the very first chapter the world is
described as without form and void, while darkness broods over
the face of the deep, and against that, as the background, is the
creation of light, leaping across the void—and upon the background of chaos arises the cosmos of order and beauty. Also at
the end of this great Book, great even as a literary production, we
have again the force of contrast, as from all the storm and tumult
of the world we are borne upwards to those heavenly spaces where
a white-robed multitude with crowns on their brows and palms of
victory in their hands, in perfect peace, chant the everlasting song.

In contrast with the apostate Church of Babylon, there is the Bride of the Lamb, Jerusalem from above, prepared as for her marriage. All through the Bible you are constantly brought face to face with the greatest possible contrasts, and much of its interest may be attributed to this source.

The same feature is stamped on this division of the Book. In the opening chapters, against the wild license and unbridled indulgence of the time of the judges, and especially against the dissolute and abominable behavior of Eli's sons, as the background, is the kneeling figure of the young Samuel, with clasped hands, engaged in prayer beneath the open sky. The beauty of the child's piety is the more exquisite because of the dark wildness, license and passion amid which it unfolds. And here, at the end of the period, where it is evident that Saul is drifting as a wreck to the rocks, while from the lurid sky the thunderbolts fall and the lightning flashes on the earth, the curtain is uplifted concerning God's own king, the man after His own heart, the young and beautiful boy called from following the sheep to be the shepherd of Israel. Against the contrast of Eli's sons you have Samuel, and against the contrast of Saul's rejection you have David's anointing. This law of contrast pervades this great book—great from the artistic and human standpoint, altogether apart from its lofty, its transcendent, its divine, origin.

We will notice the dawn of fair promise; the darkened afternoon; and, finally, the lurid gleams of a false zeal.

I. THE DAWN OF A FAIR PROMISE.—"Samuel cried unto the Lord." His intercessions rose day and night for Saul, if haply he might arrest the terrible consequences of his sin, which seemed so imminent. But he was made aware that prayer would not avail. It seemed as though Saul had already made the fatal choice, and had committed the sin which is unto death, and concerning which we have no encouragement to pray. The summons of the hour was, therefore, not to prayer but action. The Spirit of God bade Samuel go to Bethlehem and among the sons of Jesse discover and anoint the new king. Samuel was stunned by the request, and suggested that if Saul heard a whisper of such a proceeding, he would at once take measures to avenge himself by inflicting the death penalty. But the Spirit of God bade him go, taking his long horn of oil in one hand and leading a heifer with the other. Thus he made his way across the broken hill country of Judea until he came to the village of Bethlehem, lying along the slope of the hill at the foot of which, not long before, Boaz had courted Ruth. The halo of the immortal story of their love was still fresh as dew.

When he entered the little town the elders were filled with consternation; it was so unusual to see the great prophet visiting them without previous announcement. They asked if he had come peaceably. "Peaceably!" was the laconic reply. A sacrificial feast was at once prepared, the victim offered; but as some time must elapse between the offering of the sacrifice and the preparation of the food, Samuel adjourned to spend the interim in the house of the village chieftain, Jesse the Bethlehemite, a mighty man of valor and of wealth; and thus, in the privacy of the home, in a manner unlikely to attract the notice of the court, David's career as king began.

One after another the stalwart sons of Jesse passed before the prophet, and as he looked upon them in their towering stature and manly frame, he supposed that any one of them might be God's designated monarch. But his Almighty Counselor told him that outward appearance was not this time to weigh in the scales of choice; but that the royal qualities of the heart were alone to determine his selection. And so son after son passed; all had come but one, and he was with the sheep. Samuel felt that probably, because he was the youngest and the least, he might be God's accepted king. He could not proceed with the holy exercises until the boy was summoned; and, anon, coming quickly from the hills, the color mounting to his ruddy cheeks, his hair waving in the wind, his beautiful blue eyes flashing with purity and truth, David stood before the old man—the dawn of a new age, the inauguration of a better time, the keystone of the great fabric of Hebrew monarchy; above all, the man whom God loved. As his brethren stood around, the old man took the horn of oil, broke the capsule, poured it on the bright young locks, drenching them with the holy unction as the boy bent beneath. As he anointed him, it seemed as though God Almighty accompanied the outward sign and seal by the inward grace, for we are told that the Spirit of God came upon that young life from that day forward, bathing it, permeating and filling it, so that he went in the power of the Holy Spirit to meet his great lifework, to be the sweet singer of Israel, the shepherd of God's people, and the inaugurator of Solomon's temple.

You may have nothing in the outward semblance, nothing in your surroundings or circumstances, to indicate the true royalty within; but if you bare your heart to God, you shall stand revealed as His son, as a priest and king unto Himself. Oh, that at this moment the Holy Ghost might descend upon you! Would that you might seek and receive an unction from the Holy One Himself! Oh, that the Holy Spirit of God, who is the true anointing oil of the soul, might be shed upon you, so that you might go forth, saying, "The Spirit of the Lord is upon me, He hath anointed me!"

II. An Overcast Afternoon.—We have morning with David; we have afternoon with Saul. Here youth; there manhood which has passed into prime. Here the promise; and there the overcast meridian of a wrecked life.

You will notice that, whereas it is said that the Spirit of God descended upon David, we are told that "The Spirit of the Lord had departed from Saul." That does not necessarily mean that all the religious life of Saul had become extinct, but that the special faculty and power by which he had been prepared for his kingly work were withdrawn from him. It is abundantly sure that the work which a man does in this world is not wrought only by the force of his genius, the brilliance of his intellect, or by those natural gifts with which God may have endowed him, but by a something beyond and behind all these—a spiritual endowment which is communicated by the Spirit of God for special office, and which is retained so long as the character is maintained; but when the character begins to deteriorate and decline, when there is a divorce between religion and morality, when a soul turns definitely from the will and way of God to the paths of disobedience—then that mystic power, which our forefathers called unction, and which the Bible calls the Spirit of God, seems to be dissipated and to pass away as the aroma when scent has been long exposed to common air. So Saul lost the special endowment of power which had enabled him to subdue his enemies and to order his kingdom.

Secondly, we have the mysterious power of opening our nature to the Holy Spirit of God, who is the medium of communicating all the virtue, the energy and the life of God, infilling spirit, soul and body, quickening the mind, warming the heart, elevating and purifying the whole moral life. We have also the awful alternative power of yielding ourselves to the evil spirit, or demon spirits, of which the spiritual sphere is full. When we are first born into the world, the inner shrine of our being is not, as yet, occupied; it is a holy of holies not yet tenanted; but as years go on it is left for each to choose by which spirit he will be inhabited. Some, by the grace of God, are led to open their natures to receive the most blessed gift that God can bestow, since it is Himself; while others resemble Judas, of whom it is said that "Then Satan entered into him"; or Saul, of whom it is said: "Then the Spirit of God departed from him, and an evil spirit troubled him." In many cases men appear to be tenanted, occupied and infilled by the spirit of evil; and possibly even some of the worst forms of drunkenness, of lustful passion and of jealous temper, are simply to be attributed to possession by some demon spirit. In the treatment of the insane, it would perhaps be wise to bear this theory in mind and to deal with the tormented nature as our Lord did, who dealt with such as palaces occupied by legions of unclean tenants, whom He commanded to go forth.

It is affirmed that "an evil spirit from the Lord" troubled Saul. To interpret this aright, we must remember that, in the strong terse Hebrew speech, the Almighty is sometimes said to do what He permits to be done. And surely such is the interpretation here. God cannot be tempted of evil, neither tempteth He any man, but He allows us to be tempted of Satan (Job 1:6–12; Luke 22:31). Our Lord was led by the Spirit into the wilderness to be tempted of the devil, and He taught us to ask that we should not be led along that dreaded path but that the necessary discipline of life should come in some other way.

When therefore we read that an evil spirit "from the Lord" troubled Saul, we must believe that, as Saul had refused the good and gracious influences of the Holy Spirit and definitely chosen the path of disobedience, there was nothing for it but to leave him to the working of his own evil heart. The guard of spiritual help was removed, and there was nothing to prevent Satan entering him, as in after-days he entered Judas. In the solemn words, thrice repeated in Romans 1, God "gave him up" to a reprobate mind (Rom. 1:24, 26, 28).

III. The Lurid Gleams That Break Through This Overcast Sky.—In 2 Samuel 21:2 you have this: "The king"—that is David—"called the Gibeonites, and said unto them (now the Gibeonites were not of the children of Israel, but of the remnant of the Amorites; and the children of Israel had sworn unto them:

and Saul sought to slay them in his zeal to the children of Israel and Judah)." Saul was smarting under Samuel's words, writhing under the sentence of deposition, and his soul was stirred to neutralize, if possible, the divine verdict so as to still keep the favor of God. It was true, and Saul knew it well, that he had failed in one distinct act of obedience—he had kept the choicest of the spoil for himself. But why should he not, by excessive zeal in other directions, win back his lost inheritance? Granting that he has failed, he will more than compensate. Allowing that he has failed in what God told him to do, why should he not succeed in something that God had not told him to do? Why should he not resuscitate some old command and give it unexpected obedience?

Now there were two such commandments which seem to have occurred to him. The first was enacted when the children of Israel entered the Land of Promise: they should destroy all the people of the land. The Gibeonites, however, succeeded in securing that they should be excepted because they had made a covenant with Joshua, and Joshua had sworn to them (Josh. 9). The Gibeonites, therefore, had lived among the children of Israel for many centuries and had become almost an integral part of the nation. But in his false zeal for God Saul seems to have laid ruthless hands upon these peaceable people; and, in spite of the old covenant which bound Israel to respect their liberty and life, he exterminated them—an act that brought righteous retribution in afterdays on his house, for you remember how, as a setoff to this ruthless attack, Rizpah's sons, and his own five grandsons, were hanged upon a tree and left there until the rain rotted them (2 Sam. 21:8). Secondly, there was on the statute book a very drastic law against necromancers and witches, and it was commanded that these should be exterminated from the land (Exod. 22:18). Therefore Saul turned his hand against them. In his heart he still believed in them—for at the end of his life, when a man always casts aside his pretenses and appears as he is, Saul sought out one of these very women and availed himself of her help. In order, however, to show his religious zeal for God, and to extort the reversal of his sentence, Saul began to exterminate them.

But as his edicts went forth, there was rottenness in his heart. His royal state was greatly increased; he wore from this time a gorgeous turban, like other kings, which was later brought from the field of Gilboa to David. There was a great increase of luxury in his court, for he arrayed the daughters of Israel in scarlet and gold (2 Sam. 1:24). A subtle admixture of Baal worship with the recognition of Jehovah appears from his naming his sons partly from the name of Jehovah and partly by the name of Baal. He took to himself concubines in imitation of his neighbors. While on the one hand, therefore, there was this outburst of lurid zeal for God, his own heart was becoming more and more enervated and evil.

Saul's is not an isolated case. Take, for instance, two examples from the New Testament which are almost parallel. The one in which the apostle says, of Israel, that "they have a zeal for God, but not according to knowledge. For being ignorant of God's right-eousness, and seeking to establish their own, they did not subject themselves to the righteousness of God." And the other, the case of that still more famous Benjamite, Saul's namesake, who tells us that, while he was kicking against the pricks, he had a zeal for God in the persecution of the Church (Rom. 10:2–3; Acts 22:3–4).

Do not we know this in our own experience? When one has fallen under the condemnation of conscience, the heart has endeavored to whisper comfort to itself by saying, "I will endeavor to redeem my cause by an extravagance of zeal." We have plunged into some compensating work to neutralize the result of failure. It is zeal, but it is false; it is zeal, but it is strange fire; it is zeal, but it is self-originated; it is zeal, but it is only for self, and not for God; it is zeal, but it is zeal for the letter, for the tradition, for the external form; it is not the zeal of the man who is eaten up and devoured by a passionate love for the Son of God and for the souls He has made.

This is the story of ourselves. No man can get away from it. Here is the mirror in which we behold our own faces. The Bible is the Book of God, because it is the Book of man; it is the timeless Book; it is the Book that is the mirror of the soul, because man is always seeing himself in the experience of those that have preceded him.

Let us turn from Saul for a moment to that dear face that bends over us today; to that heart that yearns over us; to the Christ of God that loves us. We, too, have disobeyed, have come short, have failed to fulfill His commands, but there is forgiveness in those flowing wounds; there is pardon in that loving heart. Ask Him to blot out the past. And may the Holy Ghost kindle upon our heart-altars a fire of zeal which shall never be put out, which shall always burn for His glory, purifying our nature, making us living sacrifices unto Him.

20

"SIN BRINGING FORTH DEATH"

(1 Samuel 18:12)

"We scatter seeds with careless hand,
And dream we ne'er shall see them more;
But for a thousand years
Their fruit appears
In weeds that mar the land, or healthful store."

KEBLE

NEVER has there been a truer illustration of the words in which the Apostle James describes the genealogy of sin and her fateful family than that furnished by the life history of Saul. No sooner are we told that he had begun to yield to the spirit of evil than the historian hastens to tell us of the successive steps by which the early suggestions grew into a headlong passion, hurrying the monarch to one breach after another of the divine law. How true it is that they who offend in one point are finally guilty in all. The first sin is like the letting in of water which gradually eats away the embankment, so that presently the entire flood of waters inundates the land.

It befell thus. About this time, while Saul was smarting under Samuel's sentence of deposition, David for the first time crossed his path. Two accounts of the introduction of the young shepherd to the God-forsaken and moody monarch are given, but are not inconsistent. The one tells of his entering the royal palace as a minstrel, the other of his prowess in war, which rendered his presence an indispensable adjunct to the court.

The attacks of Saul's depression and despondency became more frequent and severe; and at last it was suggested by his servants—tradition says by Doeg the Edomite—that the effect of music should be tried on the poor diseased brain. "Behold now," they said, "an evil spirit from God troubleth thee; let our lord now command thy servants, which are before thee, to seek out a man who is a cunning player on the harp, and it shall come to pass, when the evil spirit from God is upon thee, that he shall play with his hand, and thou shalt be well."

Instantly the king fell in with the suggestion; and presently David's name was mentioned by one of the young men, who had, perhaps, come from the same part of the country and had often met the son of Jesse in their native village, may even have sat with him at the feet of the same rabbi. The young shepherd was possessed of the very qualities which were most captivating for the king. He was skillful in playing. Already he had come to be known as a man of valor in the border skirmishes which he maintained with them for the integrity of his father's flock. He was skillful in judgment and eloquent in speech. Manly beauty characterized his countenance and port. It seems as though that had happened to David which happens in measure to all God's servants—the unction and abiding of the Holy Spirit had brought out into fair and living prominence his natural traits, as when a spark is taken from common air and plunged into a jar of oxygen gas, or as though an island which had long lain under the spell of Arctic winter could be loosed from its moorings and drifted down to southern seas, and beneath the genial touch of the tropic summer all the buried seeds should burst forth into a rich and luxuriant growth.

The description given to him greatly pleased the king, who

was always on the lookout for promising youths, and in the exercise of that unquestioned autocracy which marked his reign, like that of other Eastern monarchs, he despatched a summons to Jesse to send him David, his son, who was with the sheep. Such a summons could not be disregarded, and making up a present of the produce of his farm, the old man despatched his Benjamin to begin to tread the difficult and intricate paths of royal favor. "And David came to Saul, and stood before him, and he loved him greatly." And whenever Saul was overtaken by one of his fits of melancholy, when the sky was overcast with the heavy clouds of God-forsakenness and despair, "when the evil spirit from God was upon him," David, then probably about eighteen years of age, took the harp and played with his hand, so that Saul was refreshed, and the evil spirit departed from him, and he was well.

Robert Browning has depicted for us, with a wonderful luxuriance of imagination, the scene when the minstrel strove with all the spell of his art to tame and exorcise the depression that mantled the royal brow: how he sang of the scenes in the valleys where the sheep were being gathered beside the brimming waters of the wells; and again of the pasture lands over which they were scattered, browsing on the tender grass. At one moment there was a strain of martial music, summoning the clans to repel a border foray; at another it seemed as though the voices of maidens were welcoming back from the fight their lovers, crowned with victory. Again, the music told of the rising storm, the rattle of the thunder, the pelt of the hail, until you became aware that the fury of the elements had spent itself and was dying down into the cadences of a summer landscape, bathed in peace. Now you could have heard the sough of the wind through the trees, or sweeping over the meadows, and anon the music of the spheres, as the heavens declared the glory of God and the firmament told of His handiwork. Sometimes the young poet would rehearse the joy of drinking the pure nectar of young life:

> "Oh, the wild joys of living! the leaping from rock up to rock;
>   The strong rending of boughs from the fir tree; the cool silver shock
>   Of the plunge in a pool's living water—the hunt of the bear,
>   And the sultriness showing the lion is couched in his lair.
>   And the meal—the rich dates yellowed over with gold-dust divine,
>   And the locusts' flesh steeped in the pitcher! the full draught of wine,
>   And the sheep in the dried river-channel where bulrushes tell
>   That the water was wont to go warbling so softly and well.
>   How good is man's life, the mere living! How fit to employ
>   All the heart, and the soul, and the senses forever in joy."

It is probable that the spell of music with which David sought to relieve the king's dark moods was greatly successful, as afterward in the case of Philip V of Spain, who was cured of a fixed melancholy by the music of a famous player. His fits of insanity became less and less frequent, the need for David's attendance at court was greatly relaxed, and the king may almost have ceased to think of him, amid the many suitors for his royal favor. Perhaps this very fickleness was part of the disease. It was due probably to the disordered condition of the king's brain that he well-nigh forgot the stripling whom he had greatly loved and who had become alike his armorbearer and his physician (16:21–23).

How long a period elapsed in this way we cannot tell, but another series of events brought Saul and David into closer and more tragic contact. The Philistines had never forgiven the Hebrews for having discarded the yoke which for so long they had meekly borne, and at last, after a series of forays and raids on the southern borders of Canaan, the tide of invasion could no longer be restrained. It rolled across the frontiers and poured through the valleys, till the Philistine hosts were gathered together in the valley of the Terebinth, which belonged to Judah, and pitched their camp at Ephes-dammim, "the Boundary of Blood," so-called probably, from the dark and bloody encounters which had taken place there. The valley, or wady, is broad and open, and about three miles long. It is divided in the center by a remarkable ravine, or trench, formed by a mountain torrent, which is full of foaming water in the winter, though dry in summer. It was the presence of this gorge or channel, some twenty feet wide, with steep vertical sides and with a depth of ten or twelve feet, that protracted the issue for so long, so that the two hosts lay watching each other for forty days, neither of them daring to face the hazard involved in crossing the valley and its ravine in the face of the other.

The full story of the combat with Goliath belongs to the LIFE OF DAVID; we only touch on it here as it concerns the ill-fated and hapless Saul.

When the gigantic Philistine champion, whose name was suggested by his "shining armor," strode forth, and even dared to come near the lines of the Hebrew troops, clothed in helmet, jerkin and greaves of bright copper mail, handling a mighty spear, and with a sword girt at his side; and when he boldly challenged the armies of Israel to produce a man worthy to take up the gage of battle, Saul was as dismayed and panic-stricken as any of his soldiers. It is said that he was "greatly afraid" (v. 11). Though he was God's chosen king, and in his earlier life had stood in the might of a simple faith, his disobedience had severed the sinews of his power and he had become as weak as any other. Obedience and faith are two aspects of the same posture of the soul: as you obey, you are able to believe; as you believe, you can obey. In the Epistle to the Hebrews, the fourth chapter, the words are perpetually interchanged. Let a man but have faith in God, he waxes valiant in the fight and turns to flight armies of aliens. One can chase a thousand and two put ten thousand to flight. Oh, beware of disobedience which introduces trembling and faintness into the heart, so that the sound of a driven leaf chases the fugitive! All that Saul could do, in the face of the braggart blasphemy of Goliath, was to hold out the most lavish promises of what he would do for the hero who would take up the challenge and make the proud Gittite bite the dust.

When, finally, David was brought into his presence, his soul glowing with a heroic faith, and avowing his determination to go alone to fight the Philistine, Saul endeavored to dissuade him. "Thou art not able to go against this Philistine to fight with him." He had no idea of power other than that which came of long usage (v. 33), or of helmets and coats of mail (vv. 38–39). The point of David's narrative of his successful conflicts with the lion and bear was entirely lost on him. Saul looked on them as the result of superior agility and sinewy strength; he did not fathom David's meaning as he spoke of the great deliverances which Jehovah had wrought (v. 37). Already the young Psalmist was saying to himself:

> *"The Lord is my light and my salvation,*
> *Whom shall I fear?*
> *The Lord is the strength of my life,*
> *Of whom shall I be afraid?"*

But such boasts of the believer in God were an enigma to the king. The eyes of his heart were blinded, and he could not see. He had no idea that faith opens altogether new sources of power, touches stops in the great organ of nature which elude other hands, and avails itself of those divine prerogatives which, like legions of angels, wait in harnessed squadrons around the beset believer.

As David went forth to meet the Philistine, Saul said to Abner, his uncle and the trusted captain of his army, "Whose son is the youth? Inquire whose son the stripling is"; and when presently the young champion returned with the head of the Philistine in his hand, the one question the king put to him was "Whose son art thou, thou young man?" It was as though Saul thought to account for his success on the ground of heredity. "Surely," thought he, "this youth comes from a great line of ancestry; the blood of Caleb or Joshua must be in his veins; the best of Hebrew stock must have yielded this scion." It is thus that the man of this world tries to compute and reckon up the child of faith. He is always analyzing the elements of his success and trying to account for him. He has no conception of what God can be or do for the soul that wholly trusts Him.

On the ground of expediency, after his return to Gibeah, Saul set David over the men of war. The harp was exchanged, for the most part, for the sword; and as he went forth on his expeditions against the hereditary foes of Israel he became more and more necessary to the stability of the throne—as he became increasingly the darling of the nation. "Whithersoever Saul sent him, he behaved himself wisely." Out of this popularity originated the great sin of Saul's life.

On one occasion, as Saul and David were returning from some final and decisive victory over the Philistines (v. 6, see R.V. margin), the people crowded to meet them and the troops; and the women, dressed in gay attire, danced around and before the advancing columns, singing to the music of their tambourines and three-stringed instruments. As they performed the usual sacred dance they sang responsively, "answering one to another," an ode of victory, of which this was the refrain:

> *"Saul hath slain his thousands,*
> *And David his ten thousands."*

Instantly the king was smitten with the dart of jealousy. All his soul was set on fire with the thought that not improbably David was the neighbor of whom Samuel had spoken as being the divinely designated successor to the kingdom, which was even now passing from his hand. What if this bright young soldier, with the light of God on his life and the love of the people already gathered to his person, was to dispossess him! "And Saul was very wroth, and the saying displeased him; and he said: 'What more can he have but the kingdom?'"

"And Saul eyed David from that day and forward." All the

love and admiration that he had entertained towards him turned to gall and bitterness. The milk of human kindness turned sour. His old malady, which had been charmed away from him, came back with more than its usual force; and on the day after the incident, brooding over his fancied wrongs, it seemed as though his whole nature was suddenly thrown open to an evil spirit who possessed him and swept him on to do a deed of murderous hatred. Raving in a mad fit of frenzy, he caught up the spear that stood beside him as the emblem of his royal state and hurled it at David, who was sitting before him, endeavoring to charm away his malady. Not once, but twice the murderous weapon quivered through the air; but David escaped from his presence twice, no doubt imputing the attempt on his life to the king's illness and having no idea of the jealousy that was burning in his soul like fire.

Let us take care of the first beginnings of sin, when the least suggestion begins to float in the air around us—like a microbe or germ of a malignant and deadly disease. Then is the time to turn to Christ with it for deliverance, securing His gracious interposition as you exercise faith in the grace of His salvation. "Keep back Thy servant also from presumptuous sins; let them not have dominion over me; then shall I be upright, and I shall be innocent from the great transgression."

21

THE SIN OF JEALOUSY

(1 Samuel 18)

"All selfish souls, whate'er they feign,
Have still a slavish lot;
They boast of Liberty—in vain—
Of Love—and feel it not!
He whose bosom glows with Thee—
He, and he alone, is free."

COWPER

AMONG the most terrible of human sins is jealousy—the parent of the darkest and blackest crimes that have disgraced the annals of our race. And of all the delineations of it which are frescoed on the walls of history, none is more absolutely true to life, and terrible in its graphic coloring, than this portraiture of the first king of Israel.

I. JEALOUSY OPENS THE DOOR TO THE DEVIL.—In Saul's case the interval was the briefest possible. We learn that on the morrow after the song of the women which first aroused in his heart the feeling of jealousy towards David, "an evil spirit" came mightily upon the ill-fated monarch.

There is an impenetrable wall, we believe, built by the providence of God between human souls and the evil spirits which tenant the atmosphere around us, and which are therefore called "the spiritual hosts of wickedness in the heavenlies" (Eph. 6:12), while their leader is known as the prince of the power of the air (Eph. 2:2). No spirit of evil, however malignant, can break through that barrier from his side; but it is possible for man to break it down on his. Every time we yield in thought or act to the temptations which are perpetually accosting us, we disintegrate and impair that barrier and expose ourselves to the entrance of demon influence, which adapts itself to the outward mold of our sinful desires, only investing and filling it with an intensity of passion which would otherwise be impossible to us.

This evil spirit, in Saul's case, is said to have been "from God"— a phrase which can only be interpreted on the hypothesis that God permitted it to come, and that this tragic result transpired in direct pursuance of the immutable fixtures of the universe. If a man tampers with his soul, God cannot save him from the inevitable results. Obey the law of fire and it will obey you like a dutiful slave—this is God's will and appointment; but it is also His will and appointment that, if you disobey it, it will devour your towers, palaces, treasures and homes with merciless fury. When men rebel and vex the Holy Spirit, He turns to be their enemy and fights against them. "God," says one, "must be something to us; *what* He shall be depends on what we are to Him." Go with the wind, and it beneficently wafts you forward; go against it, and your progress becomes ruinous in its deadly cost.

> *"With the merciful, Thou wilt show Thyself merciful;*
> *With the perfect man, Thou wilt show Thyself perfect;*
> *With the pure, Thou wilt show Thyself pure;*
> *And with the froward, Thou wilt show Thyself froward."*

II. JEALOUSY DEFEATS ITS OWN GOOD.—David had suddenly become the darling of the people. With almost a single bound, he had leaped into the throne of universal homage and affection.

"All Israel and Judah loved David" (18:16). In this common affection for one who was so accessible to them all, the people forgot their ancient feuds. Not only they, but the court was enamored of him. He was set over the men of war and went out with them whithersoever Saul sent him, and his promotion was good, not only "in the sight of all the people" but also "in the sight of Saul's servants," while Jonathan loved him with a love passing the love of women; and Michal, Saul's daughter, was tenderly attached to him. There must have been something of a spell in the influence of that pure, bright soul over all who came into contact with it.

Besides this, the Lord was evidently with him. Note how constantly the sacred chronicle touches that note: "Saul was afraid of David, *because the Lord was with him*" (v. 12); "David behaved himself wisely in all his ways, *and the Lord was with him*" (v. 14); "And Saul saw and knew that *the Lord was with David*" (v. 28).

Moreover, he behaved himself *wisely*, or prospered (v. 5); *wisely in all his ways* (v. 14); *very wisely*, so much so that Saul stood in awe of him (v. 15); *more wisely* than all the servants of Saul, so that his name was much set by (v. 30).

Under these circumstances, how judicious it would have been for Saul to bind the son of Jesse to himself! Admitting frankly that he was his designated successor and that he was enjoying the special favor of Jehovah, Saul might have used David for the rehabilitation of his waning fortunes. It was evidently impossible to reverse the divine choice, but he might have postponed the infliction of the inevitable sentence. Nothing could have made the king himself more popular than to have identified his fortunes and those of his family with one who could have rendered conspicuous and inestimable service to court and kingdom. Nothing could have been easier, nothing more politic. But instead of this, Saul allowed his mad passion to smolder always, and sometimes burst into a flame, until it broke out in irresistible fury and consumed the house of his life.

In the case of the higher passions of the soul, it is often easy to curb and restrain them by the introduction of considerations of self-interest and personal prestige; but it is not so with jealousy. At the shrine of this passion, which differs from the lust of the libertine and the drink-crave of the inebriate in being wholly a passion of the mind, the jealous soul is prepared to repeat the act of Palissy the potter, who tore up the very boards of his home, after having destroyed every atom of furniture, in order to prosecute the design by which he was consumed. The peace of the home; the success of some great enterprise; the happiness and prosperity of some loved one who has been the unwitting cause of jealousy; the service of God; the prospect of long, happy years of high respect if only the passion is resisted and extinguished—I have seen these, and more than these, sacrificed because jealousy has demanded its revenge.

III. Jealousy Is Very Inventive of Methods of Executing Its Cruel Purpose.—Its shape is protean. Sometimes it uses the stiletto, whose edge is so fine that you do not know you have been struck till afterwards; and sometimes the bludgeon, that knocks to the ground with one murderous blow. The poison cup, or the fine meshes of a subtle stratagem which leads the victim to inflict his own doom—such are the methods which jealousy employs.

Trace this in the history before us. First Saul, under the excuse of his malady, attempts to take David's life with his own hand. He knew that the murderous deed would be imputed to the deranged condition of his mind, and therefore, with impunity, twice launched the javelin at the minstrel who sought to charm away his malady.

Then he sought to throw him into positions of extreme peril, by inciting him to valiant deeds on the field of battle and in border warfare. As a bribe he promised him his elder daughter, Merab, whose hand should be given him in marriage as the reward of heroic deeds; and to this was added the appeal of religion, a motive more potent than any with this devout and chivalrous soul. "Saul said to David, 'Behold, my elder daughter Merab; her will I give thee to wife: only be thou valiant for me, and fight the Lord's battles.'" And then, with unsparing hand, the sacred writer draws aside the veil and recites to us the secret thoughts that were passing in that dark and evil-haunted nature—"for Saul said, 'Let not mine hand be upon him, but let the hand of the Philistines be upon him.'" We do not know the heroic deeds to which these allurements led, but it was not for want of them that the royal promise was unfulfilled and Merab given instead to Adriel the Meholathite.

The stratagem had failed, but it seemed too insidious and too likely to realize the royal purpose to be abandoned without being put to one further proof—and Michal, Saul's younger daughter, who really loved David at this time, at least, was made the guerdon or prize to allure the young, unsuspecting warrior to fresh encounters with the Philistines. The sure evidence that a hundred of these doughty foes had fallen by David's hand was the only stipulated dowry which was required, and the honor of becoming the king's son-in-law was the theme of many a hint, suggestion and open conversation between the courtiers and the young soul on whose career so much attention was being concentrated. To his servants, Saul must have seemed to be sincerely attached to David, and to desire, with genuine earnestness, to enroll him in his family; clearly he was playing a game of unusual adroitness. On the one hand, his servants really believed that the king delighted in David and wanted the alliance; on the other, "Saul thought to make David fall by the hand of the Philistines."

It was only after the plot had failed, and it seemed as though through the providence of God David was possessed of a charmed life, that Saul spoke to Jonathan his son and to all his servants that they should slay David; again hurled his javelin at him with such force that it stood quivering in the palace wall; and finally pursued him, first to his own home, and finally to Samuel's home in Naioth (see ch. 19).

Not otherwise is it with jealousy. When a wife is jealous of another woman, who may be absolutely guiltless of any attempt to influence the husband's affections; when an elder minister becomes jealous of his assistant or of a neighbor; when a person becomes jealous of the influence which another is obtaining over his friend—it becomes almost impossible to enumerate all the unkind suggestions, all the insinuations, all the wrong constructions on conduct, all the perversion of words, actions and looks through which the soul will vent its spleen.

IV. Jealousy of the Innocent Is Unable to Avail Against God.—Everything that it does has a reverse effect from that which was intended, and so far from overwhelming the rival, it extends his influence and more thoroughly establishes his throne.

It was remarkably so with David. Saul was bent on alluring him to his ruin. Through God's interposition, however, each murderous intent was foiled and became the cause of the still greater popularity of his rival. If he is set over the men of war, he prospers wherever he is sent; if he is separated from the immediate proximity of the king and permitted to go in and out before the people, the whole nation loves him (18:13,15). If he is sent to fight the Philistines, he slays not one hundred but two, so that his name is highly esteemed (v. 30). If Saul urges Jonathan to slay him, he drives his own son to a closer friendship and forces him to plead the cause of the twin soul with which his own was knit (19:1–7). Everything that is meant for ill turns out for good. The weapons that are hurled on the young life are boomerangs which return on the hand that launched them. The curses come home to roost. Saul digs privily a pit into which he falls himself.

If only jealous people would ponder such a story as this, surely they would see the uselessness of their malignant attempts to injure those who may seem destined to take their place. It is not thus that the peril can be met. The stars in their courses fight against Sisera. Balak may bribe Balaam with his wealthiest rewards to come to curse Israel, but how shall he curse whom God hath not cursed, and how shall he defy whom the Lord hath not defied?

There is a nemesis in life which will certainly return on the evildoer. The Lord will not leave His Davids to the cruel mercies of a Saul. He will raise up Jonathans to warn them of their peril, will cause Michal to ward off the molesting blow, will overpower with the mysterious spell of spiritual influences the murderous bands, and will still the enemy and avenger.

> *"God is a righteous judge,*
> *If a man turn not, He will whet His sword;*
> *He hath bent His bow and made it ready,*
> *He hath also prepared for him the instruments of death.*
>
> .   .   .   .   .
>
> *His mischief shall return upon his own head,*
> *And his violence shall come down upon his pate."*

22

"CRUEL AS THE GRAVE"

(1 Samuel 19–27)

" 'Tis greatly wise to talk with our past hours;
And ask them what report they bore to heaven;
And how they might have borne more welcome news.
Their answers form what men Experience call,
The Spirit walks of every day deceased,
And smiles an Angel, or a fury frowns."

YOUNG

JEALOUSY has no scruples and will not hesitate to violate the most revered sanctities. Her foot is ruthless; it will trample upon the relationship of home, the bonds of friendship and kinship, and the reverence which attaches itself to the house and worship of God. When once this passion has kindled, there is nothing on which it will forbear to feed, nothing is too sacred to be fuel for its flame. Not that it often, under the restraint of Christian civilization at least, proceeds to murder; rather, by whispered suspicions, by the shrug of the shoulders, the movement of the finger, the furtive look, the suggestive question, it may destroy the peace which one has in husband, wife, child or friend.

The home life is one of the most sacred institutions of our human life. It originates in the knitting of spirit with spirit, so that the twain become one; and from that union springs the dower of blessed children, sowing the world with flowers and making the race perennially young. Such a home, in David's case, was largely due to Saul's own arrangement. When Michal, his daughter, loved David, and they told him, and it pleased him, and he gave her to David to marry, it was the burst as of a new springtide to those two young lives—happy in each other's affection, though afterwards to be sadly alienated. Yet when David had evaded his javelin and fled to the security of his home, saying to himself, "My father-in-law will at least respect the sanctity of his daughter's love," the madly jealous monarch sent messengers thither to watch him and slay him in the morning, eliciting from the imprisoned singer the plaintive strains preserved in one of his psalms (59).

> *"Deliver me from mine enemies, O my God;*
> *Set me on high from them that rise up against me.*
> *Deliver me from the workers of iniquity,*
> *And save me from bloodthirsty men.*
> *For, lo, they lie in wait for my soul;*
> *The mighty gather themselves together against me;*
> *Not for my transgression, nor for any sin, O Lord."*

Michal knew her father too well to trust his clemency, warned her husband of the imminence of death, and with woman-wit (and what will not women do for those they love!) aided him to escape, with her own hands letting him down from the window. It was due to her that the newly formed home was not rendered desolate and the light of its hearth quenched.

The sanctuary of religious worship is next in importance to the home, if not superior. They stand or fall together. The one is generally the guarantee of the stability of the other. From the home as its forecourt, we pass into the house of God as our abiding place. "In My Father's house," said our Lord, "are many mansions"; and may we not suppose that human homes are included among them?

But the case of Saul shows that jealousy will break down the precincts of the sanctuary as ruthlessly as of the home. David hastened to tell Samuel of the turn that things were taking, and of the grave suspicion which was forcing itself on his soul—that Saul's attempts on his life were not the result of a disordered brain but of a wicked and murderous will. For greater security Samuel led him to a cluster of booths, perhaps woven of willow branches (a campsite called Naioth), where a number of young men were being trained for the prophetic office and were living in the fullest manifestation of spiritual power. The very atmosphere where they dwelt seemed charged with spiritual electricity.

Into this sacred assembly Saul forced three successive bands of messengers to arrest David, and finally, in hot wrath at their failure to return, came himself. In after-days it was distinctly remembered how he came to the great well, or cistern, in Sechu, and asked with peremptory vehemence for Samuel and David. When one told him, he went off to Naioth. But he was stricken down before he ever reached the place; and there, divested of his royal robes, for a second time in his life he lay on the ground in a kind of trance, which lasted for all that day and all that night (19:23–24).

We cannot read of this singular incident without being reminded of scenes in the life of John Wesley, of whom it is said, "While he was preaching on the common at Bristol a young woman sank down in violent agony, as did five or six persons at another meeting in the evening. One was a young lady whose mother was irritated at the scandal, as she called it, of her daughter's conduct; but the mother was the next who dropped down and lost her senses in a moment—and went home with her daughter, full of joy. Bold blasphemers were instantly seized with agony and cried aloud for the divine mercy, and scores were sometimes strewed on the ground at once, insensible as dead men. A Quaker who was admonishing the bystanders against these strange scenes as affectation and hypocrisy was himself struck down, as by an unseen hand, while the words of reproach were yet upon his lips." The difference, of course, between these two phenomena lay in the result. In the case of the sunken down under Wesley and Jonathan Edwards, the outcome was a change of heart and life, together with a very blessed and exalted religious experience. In the case of Saul, the experience was as the early cloud and the morning dew, which goeth away. Whatever the nature of the experience, whether physical, mental or spiritual—and probably it was the latter—it was transient and evanescent, and left him really worse than it found him, for his jealousy next threatened the life of his noble son Jonathan.

The very fountains of a *father's love and pride* dry up before the volcanic fires of jealousy and become the cause of even deeper and wider contortions. Jonathan was one of the noblest types of manhood. A truly princely soul was his. In any age, even of the most romantic age of chivalry, he would have stood easily, and by a universally acknowledged right, in the foremost rank. Whether in the court or on the battlefield, he shone as a star of the first magnitude. Grace and beauty must have adorned his person, while intrepid daring and courage characterized his behavior on the battlefield. The darling of the people, who once saved David's life from his father, the chosen ideal of the maidens and youth of his time, wise in statesmanship, true in friendship, strong in resolution, there was everything to bind his father to him, for reasons of policy as well as of paternal pride. But those considerations had no weight with Saul while jealousy of David lay heavy in the other scale. He might be, as his friend eloquently expressed it in his funeral elegy, "lovely and pleasant, swifter than an eagle, stronger than a lion," but Saul was prepared to sacrifice it all to the spirit of revenge.

It was on the monthly festival that this new vent of the volcano which raged within Saul's heart revealed itself. It was the second day, and as on the previous one David's seat was empty. Speaking of him derisively as "the son of Jesse," thus accentuating his lowly birth and ignoring the relationship that bound him to the royal family, the king asked Jonathan the reason of his absence (20:27); and when he received the answer on which the two friends had previously agreed he fell into a grievous rage. He abused Jonathan with the vilest epithets that an Eastern man can use, like someone today who vents his scorn on the mother of the object of his hate. He then insisted on David's immediate arrest and execution, and ended by hurling his javelin at his noble son who had interfered to mollify his wrath. "So Jonathan arose from the table in fierce" (and righteous) "anger, and did eat no meat the second day of the month: for he was grieved for David, because his father had done him shame."

But jealousy is also responsive to the worst possible suggestions. Of this there is an illustration in the following chapter (21). The fugitive fled this time to Nob, where Abimelech, the high priest, presided over the relics of the ancient sanctuary. The suspicions excited in Abimelech's mind by David's unescorted and hasty advent were removed by an evasive reply, and the king's son-in-law was received with all deference, supplied with bread, with the mighty sword of Goliath, and with such spiritual counsel as the ephod could afford.

The incident was reported to Saul some months afterwards, as he was encamped "on the height" (22:6, R.V. margin) above Gibeah, waiting for tidings of his hated rival, that he might at once march with his household troops, composed of trusted Benjamites, men of his own tribe, to capture and slay him. It seemed as though all the demands of the public service were set aside and accounted as the small dust of the balance so long as the vengeance of his soul was unappeased. The promulgation and execution of law, the hearing of suits, the defenses of the kingdom—all were of no account in his estimation until this one purpose was fulfilled.

In the heat of his spirit he gave vent to the complaint (and jealousy so often takes on the tone of injured innocence) that all his servants were in conspiracy against him, that no one cared for him, that Jonathan was at the bottom of David's conspiracy, and that each was cherishing the hope of his speedy downfall in order to receive possessions and promotions as the price of treachery from the hand of the son of Jesse. It was an unjust and injurious taunt. Well might the Apostle James affirm that the tongue is often "set on fire of hell." It was so here. Mad jealousy runs amuck, striking here and there with absolute disregard of all that is most precious and true in human loyalty and love. Amid the silence that followed these undeserved reproaches, Doeg narrated what he had seen on that fateful day when he had happened to be detained at the tabernacle for some ceremonial ablution or other rite, and had witnessed Abimelech's attentions to the king's son-in-law (21:7).

Doeg's malicious statement at once diverted the king's suspicions from his courtiers to the priests. Nob was not far distant from Gibeah, and a peremptory summons, after a brief interval, brought Abimelech and all his father's house, i.e., all the males of the high priest's family of the house of Eli, into the presence of the king. In unmeasured terms Saul accused the whole of them of connivance with David for the overthrow of his throne and dynasty, and would give no heed to Abimelech's mild expostulations. The high priest pleaded that, though he had done what the king accused him of, he had done it quite innocently. He had always accounted David as one of the most faithful of Saul's servants, had looked on him as being constantly entrusted with secret commissions, and had frequently made similar inquiries of God on his behalf, believing that in this he was serving the royal will. But he might as well have tried to stem the swelling of Jordan. The king's mind was made up before he began his defense. Yielding to some unholy impulse which surely must have come to him from some malign and evil spirit, and to which his disordered nature was as susceptible as it had been to the spiritual afflatus of Naioth, he said, "Thou shalt surely die, Abimelech, thou and all thy father's house."

The royal bodyguard shrank from executing the awful sentence; but Doeg the Edomite, a foreigner, with his herdsmen, had no such compunctions, but forthwith fell on the unresisting priests, who were butchered one after another until their mangled corpses were piled in heaps and their white robes were saturated with their hearts' blood.

It was a cowardly and dastardly deed, the tidings of which must have staggered the whole nation with dumfoundering horror. All good men must have felt that the foundations of society were loosed, and that neither life nor liberty was safe while such frenzy was enthroned in their monarch's breast. The black current which had caught him was bearing him ever more swiftly to his doom; a depraved heart provoked a maddened brain, and this reacted back again to his destruction.

What a warning is here that we should not yield to the first intrusion of evil, lest the thought should lead to the act, and repeated acts to the habit, and habits congeal to character, and character become set in destiny!

Jealousy is, however, *subject to strong remorse*. These scourges are the remonstrances of that blessed Spirit who allows no soul to drift unwarned to the bottomless pit. Saul was very subject to these powerful eddies in the hurrying current.

When, in an earlier stage, Jonathan reminded his father of the priceless services that David had rendered, he hearkened attentively, relented and pledged his royal oath that he should not be put to death (19:1–7).

When David spared Saul's life in the cave, near the Fountain of the Wild Goat, amid the wild ravines that border on the western shores of the Dead Sea, refusing to put forth his hand against the Lord's anointed and restraining his surprised and eager followers—touched by a generosity which was wholly unexampled in those rude days—Saul lifted up his voice and wept, and poured out the pent-up generosity which had been natural to him in earlier days but had for long been restrained. "If a man find his enemy," he said, "will he let him get away safely? Therefore may the Lord reward thee good for what thou hast done to me this day" (24:16–22).

And when again he came in search of David and pitched his camp on the ridge of Hachilah, in the southern hills, and again through David's clemency his life was spared from the fatal plunge of the spear, which would not have needed a second thrust, Saul went so far as to say before all his camp: "I have played the fool, and have erred exceedingly. I have sinned; return, my son David, for I will no more do thee harm" (26:21).

But, alas, in every case his remorse was of brief duration and failed to produce any permanent change in heart or purpose. The fire still smoldered in his soul, awaiting the least breath of air to rekindle its flames. He might exclaim, "Blessed be thou, my son David; thou shalt both do mightily and shalt surely prevail." But David dared not trust him, and said in his heart, "There is nothing better for me than that I should escape into the land of the Philistines" (26:25; 27:1).

But the cure of jealousy is clearly set forth in these terrible chapters. Without doubt Saul's surmises were well-known to all the members of his family and especially to Jonathan. Even before Saul had blurted out his threat that Jonathan's kingdom would not be established so long as the son of Jesse lived upon the ground, the heir-apparent had assured his friend that he knew the time would come when the Lord would cut off the enemies of David, every one, from the earth (20:14–15, 30–31). And later, while Saul was seeking David's life amid the ravines of Ziph, urged on in his madness by the treacherous Ziphites, Jonathan came to his friend and strengthened his hand in God, and said: "Fear not, for the hand of Saul, my father, shall not find thee, and thou shalt be king over Israel, and I shall be next unto thee; and that also Saul my father knoweth."

Jonathan, then, was even more affected by the choice of David than his father was. He was certain that he would never succeed to the throne. Respected and loved he might be, but enthroned never. But not a cloud of jealousy ever darkened the pure heaven of his love or cast its shadow on the crystal lake of his peace. Perfect love had cast out hate; we are told that "he loved David as his own soul."

If you are tempted to jealousy, do not brood over the deadly passion or allow it to grow from less to more, but arise to deal with it at once and with all the energy of your soul. Insist on loving the one to whom you have felt the unholy passion. You reply that passion is the very essence of love. It may be impossible for you to command the passion but quite possible to practice the love— since love consists primarily not in the feeling but in the doing; not in emotions but in strong acts of self-denial and service.

Learn the true character of the individual concerning whom you were beginning to feel jealous. Be on the alert to do kind acts and speak kind words. Whenever you are tempted to utter a depreciating remark, arrest the words before they cross your lips and utter some kindly ones instead. Whenever you find yourself on the point of speaking contemptuously or judging harshly, go out of your way to do some generous deed. Overcome evil with good, hatred with love. Do not wait to feel kindly, but act promptly and heartily. Go out of your way to confer a kindness. Above all, avoid aloofness. Throw yourself in that other's company; try to enter into the anxieties, trials and temptations by which his life is torn and rent; cultivate a near and close fellowship. And always offer and present yourself to God as a living sacrifice. Believe also that God does hear you, that His Holy Spirit takes part with you against the enemy of your peace, and that He who has led you to desire perfect deliverance is prepared to work in you to will and do of His good pleasure.

23

A GREAT SUNSET

(1 Samuel 25:1)

*"Life is only bright when it proceedeth
Toward a truer, deeper Life above;
Human love is sweetest when it leadeth
To a more divine and perfect Love."*

A. A. PROCTER

AT LENGTH Samuel came to his end, so far as this world, at least, was concerned; and was borne to his grave, as a shock of grain fully ripe. Though he had spent the last years in retirement, partly because of his great age and partly because of the breach between the king and himself, he had never lost the love and respect of his people; and when finally the tidings sped through the country that he had fallen upon that blessed sleep which God gives to His beloved, the event was felt to be a national calamity, so that from Dan in the far north to Beer-sheba on the southern frontier "all Israel gathered themselves together, and lamented him, and buried him."

Josephus adds this significant paragraph to the record of Scripture: "His moral excellence, and the esteem with which he was regarded, were proved by the continued mourning that was made for him, and the concern that was universally shown to conduct the funeral rites with becoming splendor and solemnity. He was buried in his own native place, and they wept for him many days—not regarding it as the death of another man or a stranger, but as that in which each individual was concerned. He was a righteous man, and of a kindly nature, and on that account very dear to God."

The impression made on his contemporaries lingered, as an afterglow, long after his sundown. Again and again he is referred to in the sacred record.

1 Chronicles 9:22 suggests that he laid the foundations of that elaborate organization of Levites for the service of the sanctuary which was perfected by David and Solomon.

1 Chronicles 26:27–28 asserts that he began to accumulate the treasures by which the house of the Lord was ultimately erected in the reign of David's mighty son.

2 Chronicles 35:18 contains a passing reference to some memorable Passover feast which he instituted and carried through.

Psalm 99:6 and Jeremiah 15:1 commemorate the fragrance of his perpetual intercessions.

Acts 3:24 and 13:20 indicate what a conspicuous landmark was furnished by his life and work in the history of his people.

Hebrews 11:32 places him in the long gallery of time, the niches in the walls of which have been filled one by one by the statues of those who have lived and labored in the power of a living faith. "The time would fail me to tell . . . of Samuel . . . who through faith . . . wrought righteousness . . ."

I. The Blessedness of His Life.—Though Samuel's career was an arduous one, it must have been fraught with the elements of true blessedness.

He was preeminently a man of prayer. This was his perpetual resort. Whether for his people or his king, for the overthrow of the Philistines or the recovery of Saul from his evil courses, he never ceased to pray—he would have counted it a sin if he had. "God forbid," he exclaimed on one memorable occasion, "that I should sin against the Lord in ceasing to pray for you." Many a sleepless night did he spend in tears and prayers for the king whom he had set up, and to whose hands he had committed the national interests as a precious charge (1 Sam. 15:11, 35; 16:1).

It has yet to be seen, and probably we shall never know until the veil of eternity is lifted, whether the world has benefited most by our prayers or labors. It is more than likely that the men and women who have poured out perpetual supplications and intercessions have, like Epaphras, worked most effectively. These have resembled mighty mountains, reaching to the skies, down whose slopes the perennial streams have poured, wreathed in rainbow vapor, and carrying the quality of the mountain soil into the plains.

All books, says an eloquent writer, are dry and tame compared with the great unwritten book prayed in the closet. The prayers of exiles! The prayers of martyrs! The prayers of missionaries! The prayers of the Waldenses! The prayers of the Covenanters! The sighs, the groans, the inarticulate cries of suffering men whom tyrants have buried alive in dungeons, whom the world may forget, but God never! If some angel, catching them as they were uttered, should drop them down from heaven, what a liturgy they would make! Can any epic equal those unwritten words which pour into the ear of God out of the heart's fullness? But these prayers have been deeds. In the words of James (5:16, R.V.), they have availed much in their working. An energy passes from the holy soul striving mightily in prayer, which becomes a working force in the universe, an indestructible unit of power—not apart from God, but in union with His own mighty energies, of whom, and through whom, and to whom are all things.

Let us pray more, especially as life advances. Let us seek to be enrolled among those who call upon His name. Let us so live that men may shelter themselves in the thought of our intercessions, as Saul in those of Samuel.

"More things are wrought by prayer than this world dreams of."

Samuel was also characterized by great singleness of purpose. He could court, without flinching, the most searching scrutiny (1 Sam. 12:3). From those early days when, as a child, the vision of his childlike purity, contrasted with the evil of Eli's house, struck on the imagination of Israel, his had been a career of stainless and irreproachable honor. The interests of his people had been his all-absorbing concern. For these he had spent himself with ungrudging devotion, and to find that he must withdraw from them in favor of another was the sorest grief of his life. The troubles which had befallen his land had only led him nearer God and bound him more tightly to his fellow countrymen; but when he discovered that they desired him to give up his position, it required all the gifts of God's grace and all the qualities of a naturally noble nature to sustain the shock with equanimity. But again his unselfishness, which had become the inner law of his life, conquered; he set himself to secure the best successor which the age could afford and humbly stepped down from the supreme place of power.

It was this beautiful humility and singleness of purpose that arrested the reverence of his people and attracted their veneration. And it was to this trait of his character that we must attribute his perception of the divine purpose. The eye must be single in its intention if the whole body is to be full of light. Sir Percivale missed, but Sir Galahad beheld, the vision of the Holy Grail, because the one missed what the other possessed.

> *"O son, thou hast not true humility,*
> *The highest virtue, mother of them all.*
>
> .   .   .   .   .   .
>
> *Thou thoughtest of thy prowess and thy sins;*
> *Thou hast not lost thyself to save thyself,*
> *As Galahad."*

Oh, to be so absorbed in a consuming passion for the glory of God in the salvation of others that we may be oblivious of ourselves, willing to take the second place, to be reckoned as of no account—able to retire from the blaze of light that falls on the stage to the twilight of the cloister, where the progress of the days is marked by the clock chimes and the incidence of the shadows indicates the progress of the sun from solstice to solstice!

Samuel was also careful to construct. When the whole land was disorganized he began to lay the foundations of a new state. Deep down in the weltering waves his careful hands laid course upon course. The time and care he expended on the schools of the prophets, his careful administration of justice during his itineraries, his appeals to the people in their great convocations, were part of a great policy which resulted in a consolidated and united people.

Do something in your life. Don't waste the precious time in criticizing others, but put a piece of solid work into the great fabric which is rising around us and on which the new Jerusalem will one day be established. To criticize others is a less efficient way of setting them right than to do the same thing as they are doing— but so much more quickly and deftly that they are led to follow your example. I like the story of the man who, instead of criticizing the garden plots of his neighbors, made his own so beautiful that those on his right and left, to the extreme ends on either side, were led, one by one, to do the same.

> *"We will not cease from mental strife,*
> *Nor shall our sword sleep in our hand,*
> *Till we have built Jerusalem,*
> *In this our green and pleasant land."*

As first of the prophets, as the connecting link between the first days of the settlement in Palestine and the splendor of Solomon's reign, by his unblemished character, by his sympathy and strength, by his evident fellowship with the God of Israel from his boyish days to his old age, Samuel won from his people the most profound veneration; and it is not to be wondered at that one of them—who owed everything to him, though he was unable to appreciate the majesty of his personality—in the supreme hour of his desperate need, when all beside had deserted him, turned for help to the great prophet, though he had been withdrawn for a considerable time from earthly scenes, and cried, "Bring me up Samuel."

II. HIS BLESSED DEATH.—Death is not a state but a step; not a chamber but a passage; not an abiding place but a bridge over a gulf. None are "dead." We should speak of the departed as those who, for a moment, passed through the shadow of the tunnel but now are living in the intensity of a vivid existence on the other side. "God is not the God of the dead, but of the living, for all live unto Him." None are dead in the sense of remaining in a condition of *deadness*. Those whom we call "dead" are those who have passed through death into the other life. They have put off their earthly tabernacle, but the tenanting spirit has passed into other scenes and activities, for weal or woe—from which it would be an effort to tear itself if summoned to return to the cares and responsibilities of this mortal existence. Hence, "Why hast thou disquieted me, to bring me up?"

Remember how the Apostle Paul describes death. He speaks of his departure (2 Tim. 4:6). His word is a nautical term and signifies the loosing of a ship from its moorings—not that it may reach harbor, but that it may go out from the harbor, on to the broad bosom of the ocean.

This is the exact thought caught by Tennyson when he sings:

> *"Sunset and evening star,*
> *And one clear call for me;*
> *And may there be no moaning of the bar*
> *When I put out to sea.*

> *"For though from out our bourne of time and place*
> *The flood may bear me far,*
> *I hope to see my Pilot face to face*
> *When I have crossed the bar."*

To recall this sonnet is to be irresistibly reminded of another of the noble conceptions of death given by this great Christian poet—one which is so exactly in keeping with the apostle's thought —when he describes the passing of Arthur thus:

> *"So said he, and the barge with oar and sail,*
> *Moved from the brink, like some full-breasted swan.*
> *That, fluting a wild carol ere her death,*
> *Ruffles her pure cold plume, and takes the flood,*
> *With swarthy webs."*

This is death. It is a moving out of the soul from the stagnant waters and containing walls of the harbor, on to the great bosom of the ocean of eternity, where there are width and space—opportunity to explore to the furthest coastlines of thought and to attain to the golden shores of the blessed isles.

Speaking of the deaths of two men whom we both knew and loved, a beloved friend of mine has quoted a poem of Bret Harte's, which is exceedingly beautiful and fitting because it so exactly expresses the desire of the man who is in a strait betwixt two, knowing that the blessedness of this mortal life is far less than that of departing to be with Christ:

> *"But lo, in the distance the clouds break away!*
> *The gates' glowing portals I see;*
> *And I hear from the outgoing ship in the bay*
> *The song of the sailors in glee.*

> *"So I think of the luminous footprints that bore*
> *His comfort o'er dark Galilee,*
> *And wait for the signal to go to the shore,*
> *To the ship that is waiting for me!"*

Remember how the Apostle Peter describes death. Speaking of his death, he uses the very word which had been employed in that memorable conversation on the Mount of Transfiguration when Moses and Elijah spoke with the Master of the decease which He was to accomplish at Jerusalem. "After my decease" (Luke 9:31; 2 Peter 1:15); the Greek word is *exodus.* There is only one other place in which that word occurs in the whole New Testament: when the reference is to the going out of the people from Egypt (Heb. 11:22).

Death, under this conception, is a going out, not a coming in. It begins. If an ending, it ends the life of slavery and pain, and opens the way into a world where the development of the soul will be unrestrained.

Let us not dread to die. With most the soul is probably as unconscious of the act of death as of that of birth. It needs but the cracking of the frail shell, the withdrawing of the thin curtain, the slackening of the golden cord of life. In all probability we shall be surprised to find that heaven has been lying all around us, throughout the days of our mortal pilgrimage, and that we had come (long before we died) into the midst of Mount Zion, had been walking the streets of the new Jerusalem, had been mingling with the innumerable hosts of angels and the spirits of just men made perfect.

The Lord justly claims the title "the Resurrection and the Life." He has abolished death and brought life and immortality to light through His gospel. We are not now left to the dim light of a surmise, of supposition, or of hesitating guesswork. We *know* that there is a life beyond death, because men saw Him after He was risen. "We are witnesses," says one of them, "of all things which He did in the country of the Jews, and in Jerusalem, whom also they slew, hanging Him on a tree. Him God raised up the third day, and gave Him to be made manifest, not to all the people, but unto witnesses that were chosen before of God, even to us, who did eat and drink with Him after He rose from the dead."

Yes, He lives, and because He lives we shall live also. He has gone to prepare mansions for us in the Father's house, and He will come again to receive us to Himself, that where He is we may be also. And in that world we shall see His face, and His name shall be on our foreheads, and, in company with kindred spirits, we shall do His commandments, hearkening to the voice of His word. "His servants shall serve Him." Even now I suppose Moses and Aaron are among His priests, and Samuel among them that call upon His name "in the solemn troops, and sweet societies" of eternity.

24

ENDOR AND GILBOA

(1 Samuel 28 and 31; 1 Chronicles 10:13)

"Earth fades! Heaven breaks on me; I shall stand next
Before God's throne; the moment's close at hand
When man the first, last time, has leave to lay
His whole heart bare before his Maker. . . ."

R. B.

YEARS had passed since David's sling had brought Goliath to the ground, and the Philistines had fled headlong at Ephesdammim before the onset of the men of Israel. A new invasion was now planned to revenge that disgrace and reestablish the Philistine supremacy over the plain of Esdraelon, which was the necessary link between the wealthy cities of the Euphrates Valley and the vast market for their wares and produce furnished by the cities of the Nile Valley. To hold that great trade route involved the right to impose very valuable taxation on the merchandise transported to and fro—hence the desire to hold its keys. The tides of Philistine invasion, therefore, poured up by the seacoast route, which was favorable for the movements of the Philistine chariots and cavalry, and a strongly fortified camp was formed at Shunem (celebrated in later days as the abode of the rich woman who so hospitably entertained the prophet Elisha) about three and a half miles north of Jezreel.

Hastily gathering what forces he could collect, Saul marched northward and pitched his camp on the slopes of Mount Gilboa, four miles distant from the invading army and on the south of the great plain. "Green plains rising from the level of the Kishon lead to the slopes of Gilboa, swelling after a time into low heights, which rise bare and stony. Behind these the many summits of the hills shoot up abruptly some five or six hundred feet, bleak, white and barren, their only growths spots of scrub oak and mountain thorns and flowers, which in spring at least are never wanting in Palestine."

The sight of the great force which was arrayed against him seems to have completely paralyzed Saul's courage. He contrasted the complete accoutrements of the Philistines with the spears and slings of Israel and "his heart trembled greatly." The heroic courage which faith might have brought him was not now possible, since the sense of God's presence was withdrawn. No rift existed in the black canopy of despair that overshadowed his terror-stricken soul. He could say with another: "Behold I go forward, but He is not there; and backward, but I cannot perceive Him; on the left hand, where He doth work, but I cannot behold Him; He hideth Himself on the right hand that I cannot see Him" (Job 23:8–9). It was to this that the terrible series of tragedies which we are now about to narrate must be attributed. The restraining grace of God, which he had so long despised and resisted, no longer strove with him, and he was left to follow the promptings of those evil spirits—"the rulers of the darkness of this world"—who, for mysterious purposes, are permitted to assail the sons of men.

True, he inquired of the Lord—for, probably, the first time after the lapse of many years; but there was no repentance or confession of sin, only abject terror and frantic despair. Therefore "the Lord answered him not, neither by dreams, nor by Urim, nor by prophets." "If I regard iniquity in my heart, the Lord will not hear me."

I. ENDOR.—At some previous period, as we have seen, "Saul had put away those that had familiar spirits, and the wizards, out of the land." He may have done this in one of those strange lucid moments when he became conscious of the strivings of God's good Spirit, or as a counteraction to the wild strivings of passion of which he was guiltily conscious—so often men seek to atone for the sins into which they have been betrayed, by some strong outward act intended as a makeweight in the other scale, or a sop to an uneasy conscience. It became clear, however, that he had no heartfelt abhorrence of the crimes he thus punished, seeing that in his own dire extremity he had recourse to the very arts he had striven to abolish, and sought from the mouth of hell the help for which he had appealed to heaven in vain.

About two miles north of Shunem—in the rear, therefore, of the Philistine army—lay the little village of Endor. It was one of those spots from which Manasseh had failed to expel the old population; and among these, the descendants of the ancient Canaanites, was an old woman who professed to be able to bring up the souls of the dead. It is likely enough that her claims were baseless. By ventriloquism and sleight of hand she no doubt simulated the voice and appearance of those who seemed to come from the other world at her bidding. If there was more than that, we do not hesitate to affirm our belief that in all ages demons have been in collusion with necromancers and spiritualists and have answered to their call. This is at the root and heart of the phenomena of modern spiritualism.

Heavily cloaked and disguised, accompanied by two trusty companions whom tradition has identified as Abner and Amasa, Saul set forth in the early hours of the night, crossed the plain, made a detour round the eastern shoulder of Little Hermon, and arrived safely at the witch's dwelling. The door opened to admit them to the house, and amid the dark weirdness of the interior, revealed by the glimmering light of a brazier, choked with smoke,

the woman was quite unable to recognize the features of the hag-
gard man who accosted her with the request that she should bring
up whomsoever he should name.

At first she hesitated, reminding him how perilous her profes-
sion was and suggesting that to give him satisfaction might cost
her life. "Behold, thou knowest what Saul hath done, how he hath
cut off those that have familiar spirits and wizards out of the land;
wherefore then layest thou a snare for my life, to cause me to
die?"

With an oath which strangely implicated the God whom he
was at that moment denying, and with a touch of his kingly prerogative, the king assured her that no punishment would befall
her for doing what he requested. "As the Lord liveth, there shall
no punishment happen to thee for this thing."

Thus reassured, the woman asked whom she should bring up;
but she must have been not a little startled when in a hoarse whisper, as of one paralyzed and awestruck by his weird surroundings, the king said, "Bring me up Samuel."

Retiring from him to a distance, the wretched woman began
her incantations, perhaps dropping a powder on the coals of the
brazier, muttering incantations in a low voice, making passes and
adjurations. But before she had completed her preparations the
Almighty seems to have interfered, sending back His faithful servant from the world beyond the pinch of death—so that the witch
might not even appear to have the credit of securing so wonderful a visitation. "The woman *saw* Samuel."

At the same moment that she recognized Samuel she seems to
have recognized Saul also. Startled and frightened for her life, she
called with a loud voice and spoke unto Saul, saying, "Why hast
thou deceived me?" Perhaps in her excited condition of soul she
was endowed with that supernatural insight which we call *clairvoy-
ance*; or perhaps there was something in Samuel's appearance so
startlingly vivid and real that she was led in that dread hour to

connect prophet and king as in years gone by; or perhaps the king in his eagerness had drawn near and had dropped the mantle which veiled his face and figure. But however it befell, she saw through his disguise and in horror-stricken tones cried, "Thou art Saul!"

Again he reassured her and asked her what she had seen.

"A majestic being, worthy to be God," she replied, "arising as if from out of the earth."

Pressed by Saul to describe his appearance more minutely, for she was beholding a mysterious form, which, though present in the same chamber as himself, was veiled from him, she said, "He resembles an old man covered with a robe." "And Saul perceived that it was Samuel, and he bowed with his face to the ground, and made obeisance."

Very touching and thrilling was the conversation that followed. I am disposed to think that it was held without the medium of the witch, and that God permitted the prophet to speak directly with Saul, as afterwards Moses and Elijah were able to speak with our Lord of His decease to be shortly accomplished at Jerusalem. It is likely that these sentences were actually interchanged between the king and his former friend and confidant to whom he had turned remorsefully in his awful agony. Do you not think that if, even then, Saul had turned to Jehovah with tears of confession and the simplicity of faith, he would have been answered according to the multitude of the divine compassions? Assuredly he would; but there was no sign of such a change of temper.

Samuel did not wait to be questioned, but sadly told the awe-struck king that, even in the other life, his misdoings had filled his spirit with unrest, so much so that he could not forbear returning to speak to him once more. "Why hast thou disquieted me to bring me up?"

Saul's answer was that of despair. "I am sore distressed; for the Philistines make war against me, and God is departed from me, and answereth me no more, neither by prophets, nor by dreams; therefore I have called thee, that thou mayest make known unto me what I should do."

But from the lips of the prophet came no words of comfort or hope. It was useless to ask of the servant the help which was denied by the Master. There was no gain in evading the fact that God Himself was on the side of David, and against the king, whose reign had begun with such fair promise. The multiplied misfortunes which had befallen him and his realm were due to his disobedience to the direct instructions issued with respect to Amalek. The sin which he had now perpetrated had put the last touch on all his transgressions. Nothing, at this hour, could stay or avert the descending avalanche. As he had sown, he must reap; as he had fallen, so he must lie. It was, therefore, revealed that the Lord would deliver Israel also with him into the hand of the Philistines, and on the morrow Saul and his sons were sure to pass into the world of spirits. The Hebrew host would be annihilated, the camp sacked, and the land left to the fate which the conquered of those days knew well how to expect.

Little wonder was it that the king fell straightway his full length upon the earth and was dreadfully afraid. He was already weak with watching and fasting through the previous day; the events of the night had completely unnerved him, and his nervous system collapsed under the terrible strain. Even the callous nature of the witch was smitten with compunction and pity. Her woman's nature was thoroughly aroused by the awful horror that lay on the king's soul. She besought him to eat. By the trust she had reposed in him she pleaded that she had some claim on his mercy, to be expended not for her but for him. "Let me set a morsel of bread," she pleaded, "before thee; and eat, that thou mayest have strength when thou goest on thy way."

At first he refused. It seemed as though he would never rise again from the mud floor on which all the glory of his manhood lay prone. "But his servants, together with the woman, constrained him; and he hearkened unto their voice. So he arose from the earth, and sat upon the bed." What memories must have passed before his mind as he sat on that divan, while the woman hasted to prepare the meal! Did he not remember the first happy days of his reign; Jabesh-gilead; the overthrow of the Philistines, not once or twice; and the love of his people? But, step by step, he saw how he had gone down from the sunlit summits to the dark valley, where the black torrent ran and the overhanging rocks met overhead. Even as a drowning man sees the whole of his previous career passing before him in a moment of time, so the whole panorama of his past must have stood in clear outline before the mental vision of the king. Then, after hastily partaking of the calf and the unleavened cakes, the three figures stole through the darkness, back to the camp.

II. GILBOA.—On the morrow there was some slight alteration in the disposition of the respective hosts. The Philistines moved towards Aphek, a little to the west of their camp; while the Israelites descended from the heights of Gilboa and took up a position near the spring or fountain of Jezreel (29:1).

Presently the battle was joined. In spite of the most desperate efforts to withstand the onset of the heavily mailed troops that were opposed to them, the Hebrews were routed and fled from before the Philistines. It is expressly noted by the historian that the lower slopes of Gilboa were covered by the wounded, whose hearts' blood bedewed the mountain pastures (31:1, R.V. margin).

Saul and Jonathan made the most desperate efforts to retrieve the day:

> *"From the blood of the slain, from the fat of the mighty,*
> *The bow of Jonathan turned not back*
> *And the sword of Saul returned not empty."*

But it was in vain. "The battle went sore against Saul." "The Philistines slew Jonathan and Abinadab and Melchishua, the sons of Saul." The flower of his army lay strewn around him; the chivalry of Israel was quenched in rivers of blood. Then, leaving all others, the Philistines concentrated their attack on that lordly figure which towered amid the fugitives, the royal crown on his helmet, the royal bracelet flashing on his arm. "The Philistines followed hard upon Saul . . . and the archers overtook him, and he was greatly distressed because of the archers." He knew what fate awaited him if he was captured while his life was yet in him. Exposed to ignominy, tortured to death, it seemed to him that immediate death was far preferable to such a fate. "Then said Saul to his armorbearer, 'Draw thy sword, and thrust me through therewith, lest these uncircumcised men come and thrust me through and abuse me.'"

The armorbearer dared not lift up his hand against the sacred person of his king, so Saul, placing his sword-hilt firmly in the earth, fell upon the point, which pierced his heart.

The narrative which the Amalekite gave afterwards to David suggests that the effort to take his life was not at once successful, and he seems to have asked this child of a race which he was once bidden utterly to destroy to give him the last, finishing stroke. "He said unto me, 'Stand, I pray thee, over me, and slay me; for anguish hath taken hold of me, because my life is yet whole in me'" (2 Sam. 1:9). It may be, however, that all this was a fabrication, intended to win David's favor, for we are told that when the armorbearer saw that Saul was dead, he likewise fell upon his sword and died with him.

The day of Gilboa was a veritable debacle. "Saul died, and his three sons, and his armorbearer, and all his men, that same day together." The next day the Philistines set to work to strip the dead, and finding the bodies of Saul and his sons they despatched their heads, armor, and decapitated corpses to be carried in triumph through the streets of their principal cities and finally to be affixed to the walls of Beth-shan. As the tidings spread, the people left the towns and villages in the neighborhood and fled across the Jordan. Roving bands followed up the victory and carried fire and sword into all parts of the land. It was the tidings of their approach to Gibeah that caused the accident to Mephibosheth. "He was five years old when the tidings came of Saul and Jonathan out of Jezreel, and his nurse took him up and fled; and it came to pass, as she made haste to flee, that he fell, and he became lame" (2 Sam. 4:4).

One brave deed relieved the somber hues of that terrible catastrophe. The men of Jabesh-gilead could not forget how nobly Saul had come to their aid in the early days of his reign; and they resolved, at least, to retrieve the royal body from the ignominy to which Philistine malice had exposed it. The valiant men therefore arose and went all night, took down the body of Saul and the bodies of his sons from the city walls, bore them reverently back to Jabesh, burnt them to conceal the hideous mutilation to which they had been subjected, buried them under "the tamarisk tree in Jabesh," and lamented with unfeigned grief this tragic close to a reign which had been once as a morning without clouds.

It is an awful thing when a man persists, as Saul and as Judas, to the end striving against God. We feel that it was a dreadful thing to do as he did; we are horrified at his temerity; we marvel at his infatuation—yet we may fall into his wicked ways and be overcome of evil as he was. We, too, may have resort to things, habits and people which we had once religiously tabooed. We, too, are liable to step back to our undoing. If a man, having felt the evil of covetousness and set himself against the love of money, after a while allows it again to invade his soul; if a man has been a slave of his appetites, and having realized their degrading tendencies, has acted, for a while, on a vow of temperance, but has gradually allowed them to resume their former sway; if after years of irreligion he has begun to be in earnest about his soul, but has again relapsed into moral apathy—is not this like Saul seeking help in the cave of the enchantress whose class he had proscribed? Such men are wells without water, clouds carried before the blast of the tempest, for whom, in the words of the apostle, is reserved the blackness of darkness forever: "For if, after they have escaped the pollutions of the world through the knowledge of the Lord and Saviour, they are again entangled therein and overcome, the latter end is worse than the beginning; for it had been better for them not to have known the way of righteousness, than, after they had known it, to turn back from the holy commandment delivered unto them" (2 Pet. 2:20–21).

25

AN EPILOGUE

(2 Samuel 1:19 ff.)

"He who did most, shall bear most! The strongest shall stand the most weak!
'Tis the weakness in strength that I cry for, my flesh that I seek
In the Godhead!—I seek and I find it! Oh, Saul! it shall be
A Face like my face that receives thee; a Man like to me,
Thou shalt love and be loved by forever; a Hand like this hand
Shall throw open the gates of new life to thee! See the Christ stand!"

R. B.

"THE Song of the Bow"—for that is the title of the touchingly beautiful elegy with which David's muse mourned over the tragedy of Gilboa—is very moving and inspiring. It seemed as though the singer had forgotten the rough experiences which had fallen to his lot through the jealous mania of the king; and passing over recent years, he was a minstrel shepherd once more, celebrating the glory and powers of his king.

> *"Thy glory, O Israel, is slain upon thy high places!*
> *How are the mighty fallen!"*

> *"Saul and Jonathan were lovely and pleasant in their lives,*
> *And in their death they were not divided."*

It makes us think of the love of God to hear David sing like that. It reminds us that God has said, "Their sins and iniquities I will remember no more." Here at least, long before the Christian era, was a love that bore all things, believed all things, hoped all things, endured all things, and never failed; which cast the halo of its idealism around the memory of the departed; which thought only of what had been noble and beautiful in them, and refused to consider anything that had been base and unworthy. It is thus that we also would think of Saul, the first king of Israel.

·   ·   ·   ·   ·

It always seems to us as though Saul was one of those castaways of whom the apostle speaks, and among whom he feared lest he should finally be classed—who were once selected by God for some high and holy purpose, who seemed likely to realize it, but who at last were cast aside from His use and service as salt which has lost its savor and was cast out to be trodden under foot of men.

It is a very solemn thought! No career could begin with fairer, brighter prospects than Saul had, and none could close in a more absolute midnight of despair; and yet such a fate may befall us, unless we watch, and pray, and walk humbly with our God.

We cannot forget that representation on the pages of John Bunyan's *Pilgrim's Progress* of the man in an iron cage. The man said, "I once professed my faith with flourish, both in mine own eyes and also in the eyes of others. I thought I was fair for the Celestial City, and had then even joy at the thought that I should get thither. But I left off to watch and be sober; I laid the reins upon the neck of my lusts; I sinned against the Light of the World and the goodness of God. I have grieved the Spirit, and He is gone. I tempted the devil, and he has come to me. I have provoked God to anger, and He has left me. I have so hardened my heart that I cannot repent." "Well," said Christian, "this is fearful! God help me to watch and be sober, and to pray that I may shun the cause of this man's misery!"

But those who are most fearful of falling into such a case are they who are least liable to do so. The disciple who says, "Lord, is it I?" in lowly distrust of himself is he who will never be found guilty of treading the Son of God beneath his feet or crucifying Him afresh.

. . . . .

But, deeper than all, the dispensational aspect of Saul's reign appeals to us with profoundest interest. He seems to represent the prince of this present age (or, as it might be called, "the world"), who was once Lucifer, the Son of the Morning; who was appointed as God's vicegerent to rule over His heritage; who fell from his high estate, and in his fall dragged down not only a noble retinue of bright and beautiful spirits but cast a blighting influence over the entire realm over which he had been set. In each of these points there is a close analogy between Saul, the king, and Satan, the fallen archangel. Both were favored above most; both began with high promise; both were vicegerents over God's heritage; both were disobedient, willful and proud; both fell from their primal estate, and in their fall dragged many in their train, and left an entail of woe as their legacy and memento. And both incurred the sentence of deposition in favor of another kingdom which was springing up in the heart of their kingdom. In the case of Saul, this was David's; in the case of Satan, it is that kingdom which can never be removed, but abideth forever!

That gathering to the Cave of Adullam of all who were in desperate circumstances until, by careful discipline and the infusion of his own heroic spirit, David molded them into a great army and won the empire of that time and land; that generous and noble disposition which stood out in such striking contrast to the character of his adversary; that incessant persecution and pursuit by the crowned prince of the realm—what are these but striking analogies which have their highest counterpart only in the history of the Son of Man, who from His cradle to His grave was always subjected to the hatred and opposition of Satan!

Notwithstanding all that Saul's malice could do to thwart and frustrate the divine plan, yet Jehovah set His king upon the holy hill of Zion, and He openly proclaimed the fact of David's enthronement and coronation. Similarly the divine purpose with regard to our Lord must stand, though demons and men oppose it. The Son of God is destined to be the crowned King of men. His kingdom is now hidden and in mystery; His followers are not manifested to the eyes of men; the full proportions of His empire are concealed. It has yet "to come." The overthrow of its great antagonist must precede its establishment. For the universe also there is to be an Armageddon, just as there was a field of Gilboa, and only when that last fight has been fought, and the powers of darkness have been shattered, never to be reconstructed, shall there be heard the sound of many voices, as of the tumultuous sound of vast multitudes, saying, "Hallelujah, the kingdoms of this world have become the kingdom of our God and of His Christ, and He shall reign forever."

"Wherefore, receiving a kingdom, that shall not be removed, let us have grace, whereby we may serve God acceptably, with reverence and in godly fear, for our God is a consuming fire."

The reign of Saul would be almost too bitter to contemplate unless under its rough cuticle and rind we could detect the formation of the luscious fruit of David's kingdom, destined to sow eternal seed over the world. Similarly we might despair of the condition to which the Trinity of Evil has reduced our world, did we not know that in the days of these kings the God of Heaven will set up a kingdom which will never be destroyed, nor will the sovereignty thereof be left to another people; but it will break in pieces and consume all these kingdoms, and it will stand forever (see Daniel 2:44).

.   .   .   .   .

Samuel the Prophet thus practically bridges the gulf between

Samson the Judge and David the King: and there is deep significance in the fact that his name is identified with the two books of
Scripture which describe this great transitional period, every event
of which was affected by his influence.

This book was produced by CLC Publications. We hope it has been helpful to you in living the Christian life. CLC is a literature mission with ministry in over 50 countries worldwide. If you would like to know more about us, or are interested in opportunities to serve with a faith mission, we invite you to write to:

CLC Publications
P.O. Box 1449
Fort Washington, PA 19034